Staff

Original Editor: Tamami Miyazaki

Photography: Mari Harada (st. dunk)

Book design: Yoko Kitahara

Illustrations: Kiyomi Sakai

Translation: Maya Rosewood
Production: Hiroko Mizuno
         Risa Cho

Lady Boutique Series No. 3001
Kami de Tsukuru Bunbougu to Zakka
Copyright © 2010 BOUTIQUE-SHA, Inc. All rights reserved.
Translation © 2013 by Vertical, Inc.
Published by Vertical, Inc., New York.
Originally published in Japan by BOUTIQUE-SHA, Inc.

ISBN: 978-1-939130-08-2

Manufactured in Singapore

First Edition

Vertical, Inc.
451 Park Avenue South, 7th Floor
New York, NY 10016
www.vertical-inc.com

Contents

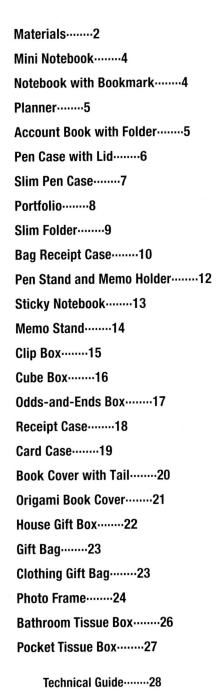

Materials

This book uses color drawing paper as well as ready-made goods such as envelopes or file folders.

Such items are easy to work with and offer additional functionality which adds to their appeal.

If you find some interesting materials, try turning them into stylish finished products.

Material

Envelopes

Products

Receipt Case p 18

Card Case p 19

Bag Receipt Case p 11

Slim Folder p 9

House Gift Box p 22

Gift Bag p 23

Clothing Gift Bag p 23

Material

● Notebooks ●

Products

● Mini Notebook p 4 ●

● Notebook with Bookmark p 4 ●

● Planner p 5 ●

● Account Book with Folder p 5 ●

Material

● Doilies ●

Products

● Gift Bag p 23 ●

● Clothing Gift Bag p 23 ●

Material

● Flat File Holder ●

Products

● Bag Receipt Case p 10 ●

● Slim Pen Case p 7 ●

Material

● Clear Folder ●

Products

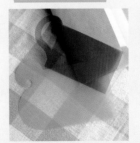

● Book Cover with Tail p 20 ●

● Account Book with Folder p 5 ●

Heavy stock is used as a cover for the notebook.

Using notebooks

01 : Mini Notebook

02 : Notebook with Bookmark

These are small notebooks that you can carry
anywhere in your pocket. Just add a cover to create
a sturdy notebook with that hardcover feel.

Instructions **01: See p 32 for instructions and photos of the process.**
02: See p 34

Add a waxed cord
for a bookmark
for version 2.
It's so simple!

It's easy to carry
these notebooks
around because
the covers are so
durable.
What should I write
about today...?

Clock: AWABEES

03 : Planner

Adding contact paper to the cover of your planner helps it withstand heavy daily use. Use a design or pattern that you won't tire of.

Instructions p 34

Add clips to both ends of a piece of ribbon to create a bookmark for an extra bit of ingenuity.

04 : Account Book with Folder

With an account book this adorable, you'll look forward to opening it each day. Put a little extra effort into the cover and add a bookmark for ultimate usefulness. Add contact paper to the outside.

Instructions p 35

Add a clear folder to the inside cover so you can stow receipts, etc.

05 : Pen Case with Lid

This is a pen case with a lid made from color construction paper or textured paper stock. This secure, sleek case is so sturdy no one will believe it's made of paper. They're so easy to make and hold so much—a real joy.

Instructions **p 36**

Close

Wrap the band around the button to close.

05

Ruler: AWABEES Newspaper: EASE

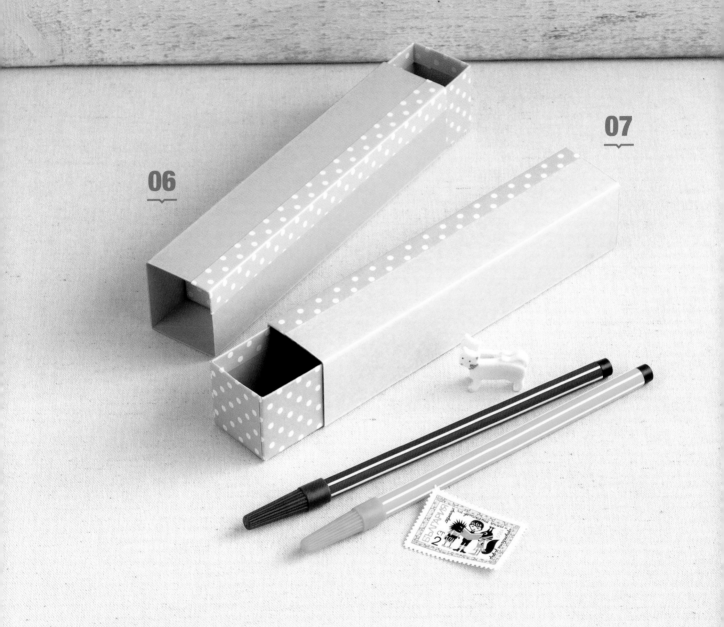

06

07

Using a flat file holder

06, 07 : Slim Pen Case

This interesting pen case is like an elongated match box.

The slim design makes it easy to carry and isn't too bulky for a bag.

Use a pop color that will lift your spirits.

Instructions   p 38

08 : Portfolio

A portfolio is the ideal way to store illustrations or other papers you don't want creased or folded. Use stiff paperboard to create a durable way to transport important papers.

Instructions **p 40**

08

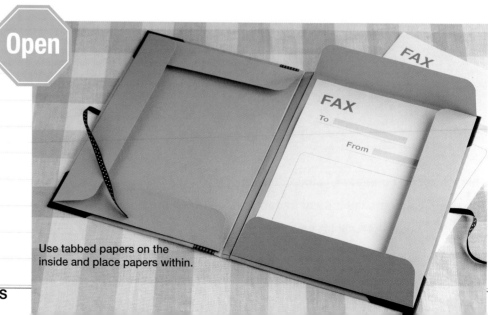

Use tabbed papers on the inside and place papers within.

09 : Slim Folder

Fold a large sheet of textured
paper in half to create a
slim-line folder.
Since these are quick and
easy to make, try making
several in different colors for
different subjects.

Instructions **p 39**

09

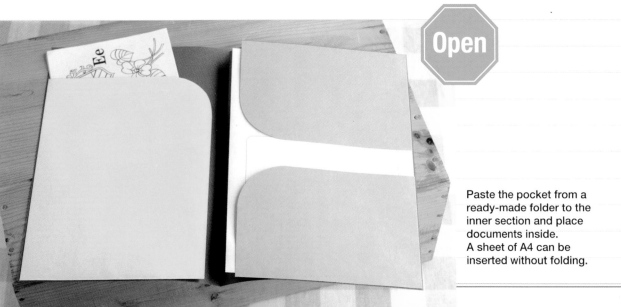

Open

Paste the pocket from a
ready-made folder to the
inner section and place
documents inside.
A sheet of A4 can be
inserted without folding.

10, 11, 12 : Bag Receipt Case

These cases, made to look like designer handbags, pack a punch!

These whimsical receipt cases are made using one flat document holder.

Use them to keep track of receipts for yourself or use as gift bags for presents.

Instructions   p 42

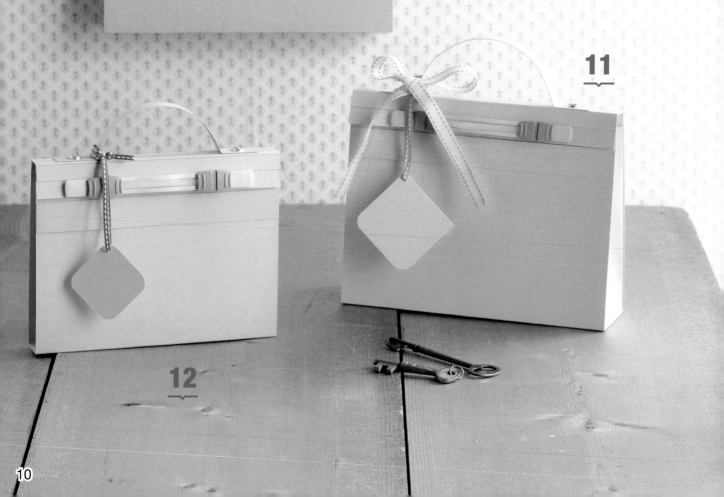

10

11

12

10 is the perfect size for keeping A5-size papers. Also perfect for keeping track of receipts.

Since **11** has no inner dividers, try using it as a gift bag, too.

12 is the perfect size for keeping seasonal cards or postcards. It's so cute and small.

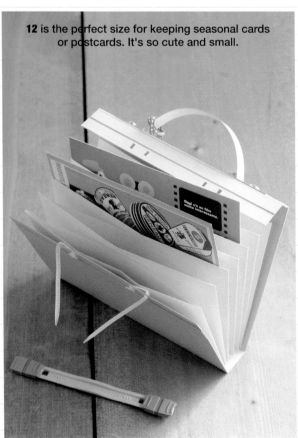

Add ribbons or tags to the handle for a stylish twist. The insides all use ready-made envelopes.

13 : Pen Stand and Memo Holder

A memo holder with a handy pen stand is a must-have
on an office desk or by your phone.
Add ribbon to step up the design aspect, and you'll
have a smart, functional memo set.

Instructions **p 44**

Make the stand to fit the size of the memo pad you'll use.

13

Using color construction paper

14 : Sticky Notebook

14

Keep a variety of sizes of sticky notes inside
this strawberry-chocolate-themed booklet.
Having this stylish and convenient notebook will
make you want to show it off to your friends.

Instructions   p 46

Open

Stick all kinds
of sticky notes
inside.

15, 16, 17 : Memo Stands

Use these memo stands to display postcards or keep quick scribbles handy. These appealingly simple stands only require decorative twist ties and some construction paper.

Instructions p 41

18, 19 : Clip Box

Clips always end up scattered all over
the place when tossed in drawers.
Keep those clips neatly stowed in
these colorful boxes.

Instructions   **p 45**

Use a magnetic sheet on the underside of the lid for **19**.
This makes it easier to retrieve clips.

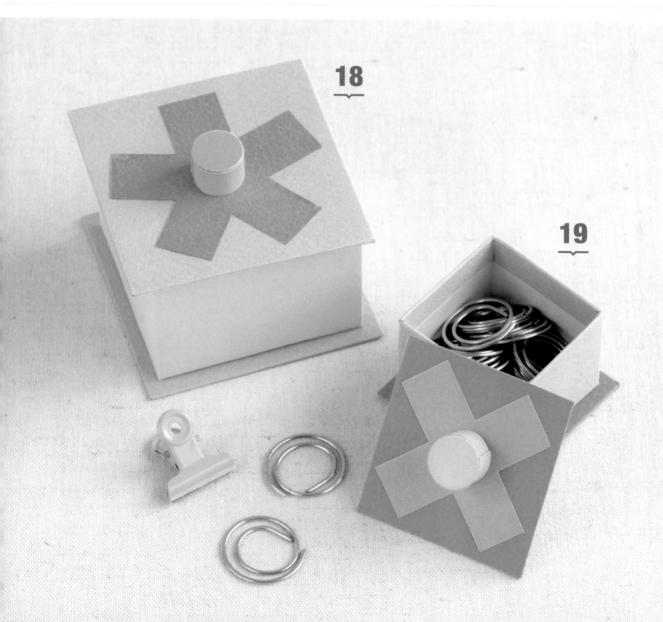

18

19

20

21

Choose the type of button and the color
of the paper to create a lovely box that's
exclusively yours.

Close

20, 21 : Cube Box

These cute cubes can be used for
all sorts of things on your desk.
You could even hide sweets in one
box for a secretive way to snack
during the workday.

Instructions   **p 47**

22 : Odds-and-Ends Box

Vivid orange plus randomly-arranged ribbon equals a very smart odds-and-ends box. This is very easy to make, as it's basically just a box. The lid makes it very functional.

Instructions **p 48**

Open The detachable dividers help keep everything neatly organized.

22

Pen, Ink: EASE

Add mini card-sized envelopes as well as large dividers.

Using envelopes

23, 24 : Receipt Case

I based this smart receipt case design on a non-folding wallet.

It's so close to the real thing no one will think it's made from paper!

This makes organizing receipts easy and fun.

[Instructions] **p 50**

Open

It's very easy to repurpose ready-made envelopes for use as dividers.
Air mail envelopes make it even more classy.

25, 26, 27 : Card Case

Store cards, insurance cards, prepaid cards...

This functional yet adorable card case will keep all your

essential cards handy and organized.

Instructions **p 52**

Open

Use ready-made envelopes as dividers.

Use contact paper for **26** and **27** for added practicality.

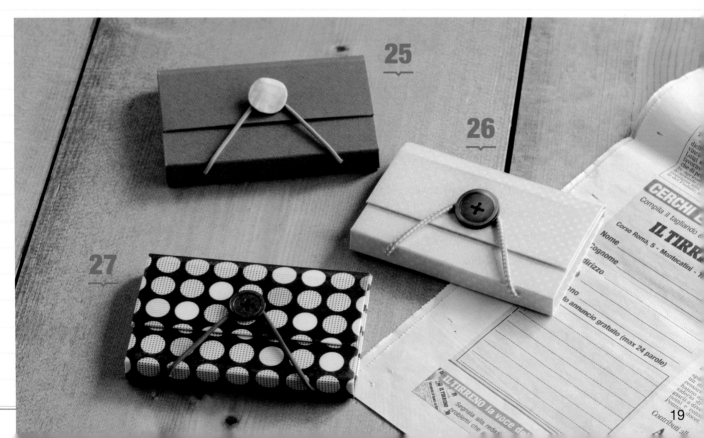

25

26

27

28

29

Using kraft paper

28, 29 : Book Cover with Tail

These book covers with cats and squirrels fit mass-market paperbacks. The bookmarks have cute curly tails which will make reading in a cafe even more enjoyable.

Instructions p 54

Use these tails, made out of clear folders, as bookmarks. The cover can be easily adjusted to suit any size of book.

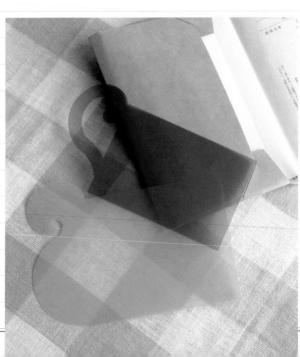

These are even more practical with
the addition of a flat elastic band.
The bookmarks have a sweet animal theme.

30, 31 : Origami Book Cover

Use your favorite paper for an origami book
cover. Once you learn the folds, you can make
covers for books or notebooks of any size.
When not used, tuck the bookmark away
into the center of the cover.

Instructions p 58

30

31

21

Tuck in the top of the "roof" to seal.
Open **32** by pulling the ribbons.
33 uses ribbon as a handle.

32, 33 : House Gift Box

These simple, smart house-shaped gift boxes are made
using ready-made envelopes and masking tape.
Use heavier paper to reinforce the insides so there's
no need to worry about the shape collapsing.
These cute gift boxes will surprise and thrill the giftee.

Instructions   **p 56**

34

35

Open

Seal the top with double-sided tape and unstick to open.

Using envelopes and doilies

34, 35 : Gift Bag

Gift bags made from colored envelopes.
The pretty top is made from a doily reinforced with heavy drawing paper.

Instructions   **p 59**

Using envelopes and doilies

36, 37 : Clothing Gift Bag

Prim yet fashionable gift bags.
You can make your own envelopes out of any paper you like and then turn them into gift bags, too.

Instructions   **p 57**

36

37

Remove the ribbon and doily to retrieve contents.

Open

Using poster board

39 : Bathroom Tissue Box

This cube box, just like the version used
on desks and tabletops, is very convenient
and doesn't take up space.
Make these boxes in all kinds of fun
patterns and colors.

Instructions **p 60**

Inside

Use heavy paper and
rubber bands to create a
simple spring that pushes
up the roll as it runs low.

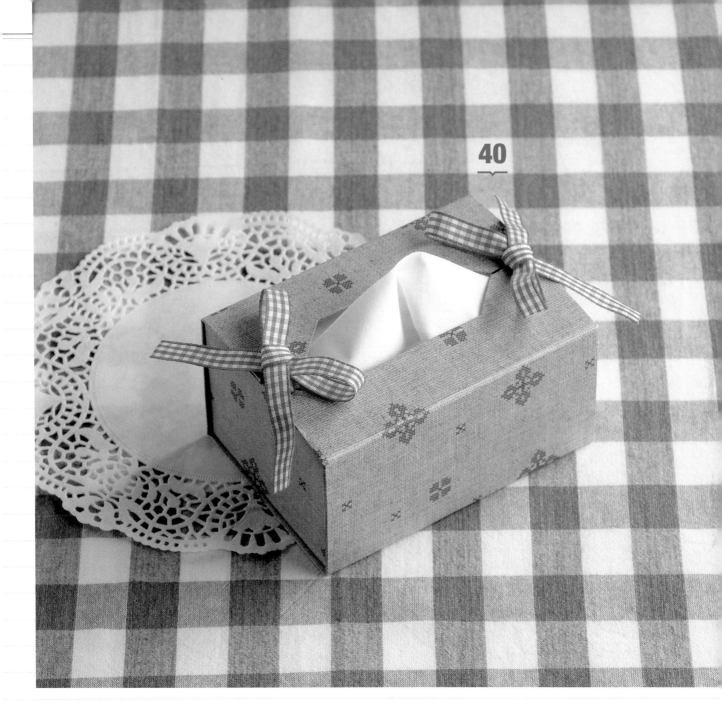

40 : Pocket Tissue Box

Place pocket-sized tissue packets into this neat,
easy-to-use box. Just pull out the inner box like a
drawer and place tissues inside.

Instructions　**p 63**

Technical Guide

Here we'll introduce techniques you should know for creating handmade paper goods.

Supervisor: Keiko Komatsubara

Materials Used in this Book

Foundation Paper

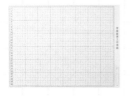

Heavyweight Construction Paper

This thick paper can be used as a base for all the designs. With the grid, you can easily cut the sheets to any size.

Color Construction Paper

Use durable, heavyweight construction paper that can stand up to scoring and folding. Finer-quality papers have a nice sheen that lends nice color to finished products.

Posterboard

Paperboard

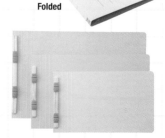

Posterboard/Paperboard

These heavy-duty papers can be used in any design. Paperboard is the sturdier of the two. Some varieties of posterboard are gray on one side.

Folded

Flat Document Holders

These folders are normally used to store documents, but the heavy-duty paper colored on both sides makes them perfect for use in these designs. These are like paper-based clipboards. The plastic clips can also be used in some designs.

Decorative Papers

Textured Paper

Heavyweight paper with a texture similar to fish scales. Mostly used by pasting to a base of construction paper. If the textured paper will be on the outside of a finished object, use thinner paper.

Patterned Paper

12" x 12" sheets that are used for scrapbooking. Mostly used by pasting to a base of construction paper. A wide variety of patterns are available. It's on the thin side and relatively easy to use. (Provided by: Kuretake)

Kraft Paper

Light-brown thin paper that's especially useful in designs intended to look like household goods. They come large, so cut the paper into the size needed for the design.

Waterproof Wrapping Paper

Originally for packing, typically with a lattice pattern of threads inside. The surface has a sheen and is used in designs intended to look like household goods.

Wrapping Paper

Thin paper used to wrap presents, etc. Available in a variety of patterns, such as text, flowers or geometric shapes.

Other Papers and Sheets

Bristol Paper

This paper is smooth and resilient. This book uses Bristol paper in combination with doilies.

Doilies

Typically found in round shapes with lace patterns around the edges.

Contact Paper

Clear film used to finish the covers of handmade notebooks. It creates a sturdy, waterproof finish.

Comes with protective non-adhesive paper on the back.

Envelopes

Used as dividers in folders or receipt cases. You can use all kinds, from business-use sizes for A4 or B5 letters to air mail and card envelopes.

Clear Folders

Used to keep documents organized and separated. Can be easily cut with scissors or a craft knife into bookmarks or a variety of other objects.

Ribbons, Tyrolean Fabric Tape
Used as accents on finished goods. Available in a wide range of colors and widths.

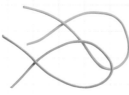

Hair Elastic
Use with a button to create a simple clasp.

Flat Elastic
Use to anchor book covers.

Waxed Cord
Use as a bookmark or to wrap up receipt cases.

Buttons
Use with elastic to create a simple clasp.

Masking Tape
Can be easily removed. Patterned versions can be used as decoration.

Clips
Use as bookmark ends or to clip paper. Available in a range of styles. (Provided by: Kuretake)

Brads (Fasteners)
Place through a punch hole and spread the two ends to fix in place. Available in a variety of colors. (Provided by: Kuretake)

Craft Punch
Tools that can create unusual hole punches in paper. Available in a wide variety of shapes.

Magnetic Sheet
Sheet-style magnets that can be cut with scissors. Sold in craft or dollar stores.

Decorative Twist Ties
Wire-based ties that were originally used to tie off bags. Sold in craft or dollar stores.

Notebooks
Use in making original notebooks. Can also be used as journals or account logs.

Sticky Notes
Memos that can be stuck and restuck on other surfaces. Use in making the Sticky Notebook.

Memo Pad
Use in making Pen Stand and Memo Holder. Choose any type you prefer.

 **Tools You'll Need**

Scissors
Use to cut ribbon, etc.

Pinking Shears
Scissors that create a zig-zag line.

X-Acto or Craft Knife
X-Actos can be used for general paper cutting. Craft knives are best for cutting curved lines or complex designs. This book uses these for cutting all paper.

Ruler
Use a carpenter's square for ease in cutting paper. Long rulers are convenient when drawing guidelines on paper.

Spatula
Use to smooth out surface of paper after pasting. The one pictured is used to stick screentone to paper.

Glue
Use on textured or other heavyweight paper. Gives a stronger bond than double-sided tape.

Tweezers
Use when handling or glueing small parts.

Needle and Thread
Use to affix buttons to paper.

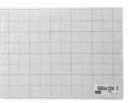

Cutting Mat
Use under paper when cutting with a craft knife.

Cellophane Tape
Use to tack together pieces of paper when creating objects.

Hole Punch and Wood Mallet
Hole punches create round holes. This book uses 4.5 mm and 2 mm punches. Strike punch with wood mallet to create holes.

Double-Sided Tape
Tape that acts like glue. Try getting a variety of widths to use, but pick a wide one if you can't.

Double-Stick Sheets
Sheets are easier to use when sticking together large surface areas, such as with handmade notebooks. Lined on both sides with protective paper. Sticks paper quickly.

Awl
Use in place of a hole punch to open holes in paper.

Cylindrical Pencil
Use to add curves to paper. Roll pencil (or cylindrical pen) across paper to curl.

Folding Paper

For thin to medium-weight paper

01 Place ruler along line for valley fold and score using the back of the craft knife.

02 For mountain folds, score along the reverse.

03 Valley fold along the scored line by hand to create the fold in the paper. Done!

For heavyweight paper

01 Place ruler along line for valley fold and press hard while scoring using the back of the craft knife.

02 With the ruler still in place, fold paper up along the line. If it's too stiff, score along the reverse (over the mountain fold).

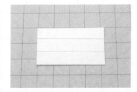

03 Done!

Working with Double-Sided Tape

When covering a surface

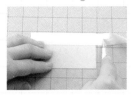

01 Using 3/4" width tape, place top left corner flush against paper. Leave a small margin on the right.

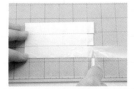

02 Continue adding strips of tape until paper is covered.

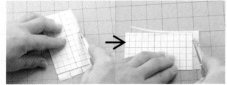

03 Flip over paper and slice off excess tape around edges with a craft knife.

04 Double-stick tape is now adhered to the entire paper.

Working with a narrow piece of paper

01 Using 3/4" tape, stick tape to the paper from above.

02 Snip off tape and flip over.

03 Slice off excess tape around edges of paper with an X-Acto.

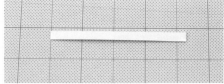

04 Done! This method is convenient when the tape is too wide for the paper or if you only have wide tape.

Working with double-stick sheets

01 Both sides should have protective paper. Partially peel back the protective paper on one side and place the craft paper you're working with on it.

02 While pressing the craft paper down, slowly peel off the protective paper.

03 The paper is now stuck to the sheet.

04 Slice off excess tape around edges of paper with a craft knife.

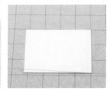

05 Now the double-stick sheet is trimmed to the size of the paper. Peel off the other layer of protective paper before use.

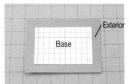

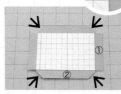

01 Adhere base paper to exterior paper with double-sided tape. This book uses 1.5 cm margins unless noted otherwise.

02 Remove equilateral squares from all four corners of exterior paper.

03 Using a paper triangle ruler (see p 33), cut margin corner at a 45° angle. (Align ruler 2 mm from base paper.)

04 Repeat with remaining corners on the top and bottom edges of the margin. (See inset photo.)

05 Score along outer edge of base paper to crease exterior paper.

06 Glue along margins. Start with the uncut edge (marked ①).

07 Prep a paper spatula (see p 33) and spread glue from the inside to the outer edge.

08 Adhere margin to the base paper. Press with a spatula to create a nice finish.

09 Having adhered the uncut edges, glue and fold the remaining edges as well.

10 Done! In most cases, margins are affixed with glue, not double-sided tape.

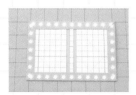

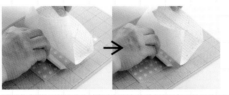

01 Prepare the cover for the handmade notebook. This demo uses the cover shown on p 32 (see p 32, steps 1-6).

02 Place contact paper with protective paper face up on a clean cutting mat. Peel protective paper back slightly and place cover on top.

03 Flip over. Using a spatula, slowly press the contact paper from the near to the far side while peeling off the protective paper.

04 Now the contact paper is on the cover. The excess contact paper is adhered to the cutting mat.

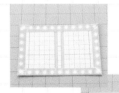

05 Following the directions on the instruction page, slice off excess contact paper, leaving the specified amount to create margins.

06 Remove equilateral squares from all four corners of excess contact paper. Using a paper triangle ruler (see p 33), cut top and bottom margin corner at a 45° angle. (Align ruler 2 mm from base paper.)

07 Fold margins over, starting with the uncut ends.

08 Once all margins are folded, smooth with a spatula to reinforce adhesion.

09 Done!

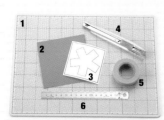

01 Prep materials and tools.

1. Cutting mat
2. Paper for pattern
3. Pattern
4. Craft knife
5. Masking (or cellophane) tape
6. Ruler

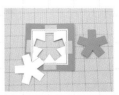

02 Place pattern on top of paper and tape on all four sides.

03 Cut along lines of pattern, starting at the far side and working in. A ruler helps when cutting straight lines.

04 Done!

Materials

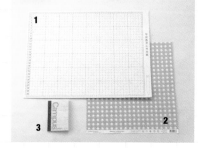

1. 1 sheet construction paper (A3)
2. 1 sheet patterned paper (instructions use a different pattern than the finished product shot)
3. A7-sized notebook

Tools

1. Cutting mat
2. Glue
3. Double-sided tape
4. Craft knife
5. Spatula

Instruction

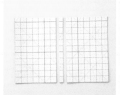

01 Cut construction paper into 2 pieces sized 10.7 x 7 cm and 1 piece 10.7 x 0.7 cm. The narrow piece will become the spine.

02 Cover all pieces with double-sided tape (see p 30 for instructions).

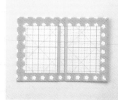

1.5 cm
Patterned paper (reverse)
1.5 cm

03 Cut patterned paper to 13.7 x 18.7 cm. Flip over. Draw guidelines 1.5 cm from the left and bottom edges.

5 mm   5 mm

04 Peel protective paper off of paper from step 02 and adhere to patterned paper along the guidelines.

05 Create margins (see p 31, steps 1-5).

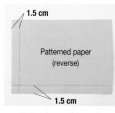

06 Glue margins and adhere to construction paper (see p 31, steps 6-10).

07 Use spatula to crease along inner edges of the spine.

08 Fold up so the front is facing out. Press sides of spine so they cave in slightly.

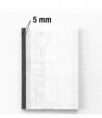

5 mm

09 Stick double-sided tape to front and back covers of the notebook, leaving 5 mm from the spine on both sides uncovered.

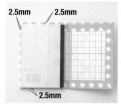

2.5mm   2.5mm
2.5mm

10 Unfold paper cover. Peel off protective paper from one side of the notebook and press into cover, leaving a 2.5 mm margin on 3 sides.

11 Peel off protective paper from other side of notebook and fold new cover on top, making sure to keep it aligned.

12 Done!

Production Hints

Envelopes

Envelopes are very handy for use in making papercrafts. They can be used as dividers in receipt or card cases or the foundation for gift boxes. Here we'll introduce the business envelopes used in this book.

Rectangle (Opens on short end)

◉ **Kaku #2 (240 x 332 mm) (Appx 10" x 13")**
  Fits A4 paper

◉ **Kaku #3 (216 x 277 mm) (Appx 8.5" x 11")**
  Fits B5 paper, journals, magazines, etc.

◉ **Kaku #4 (197 x 267 mm) (Appx 8" x 10.5")**
  Fits official notices

◉ **Kaku #6 (162 x 229 mm) (6 3/8" x 9")**
  Same as C5. Fits A5 paper

Western

◉ **You #2 (162 x 114 mm) (6 3/8" x 4 1/2")**
  Same as ISO C6.
  Fits A4 folded into quarters.

Long

◉ **Chou #4 (90 x 205 mm) (Appx 4" x 8")**
  Fits B5 folded into quarters

Paper Rulers and Spatulas

Rulers are needed to measure angles and widths. This book uses a few standard angles and sizes. Margins use 45° and 90° angles and widths of 1 and 1.5 cm.
Prep these rulers and guides to make measuring so much simpler!

Triangle Ruler

45°
45°   90°

Can be made by cutting a square piece of thick paper in half on the diagonal. Write in the angles on the three corners.

Width Guides

1 cm

1.5 cm

Make guides for 1 and 1.5 cm widths. Simply place along the margins and cut to width.

Paper Spatula

Use the scraps from making objects and cut into rectangles to make disposable spatulas for spreading glue.

Legend for patterns

Here are the symbols used in the instructions for the products starting on page 34.

* All measurements are listed as length x width. E.g., 10 x 5 cm = length 10 cm x width 5 cm

—·—·—·—·—·—·— → Mountain Fold   — — — — — — — — → Valley Fold

━━━━━━━━ → Cut

▧ → Place double-sided tape or glue here

Page 4, #2 Notebook with Bookmark

● Materials ●

Construction paper.....	A3	Gray	1	
Kraft paper.....................	A4	Light brown	1	
Button.............................	1 cm diam.	White	1	
1 mm Waxed cord	25 cm	Red	1	
Notebook	B7	———	1	
Sewing thread...............	as needed	Black	1	
Ribbon (9 mm wide)....	40 cm	Navy/red check	1	

● Tools ●

Craft knife
Cutting mat
Scissors
Double-sided
  tape (3/4")
Glue
Cellophane tape
Spatula

· Guidelines and sizes for the construction paper

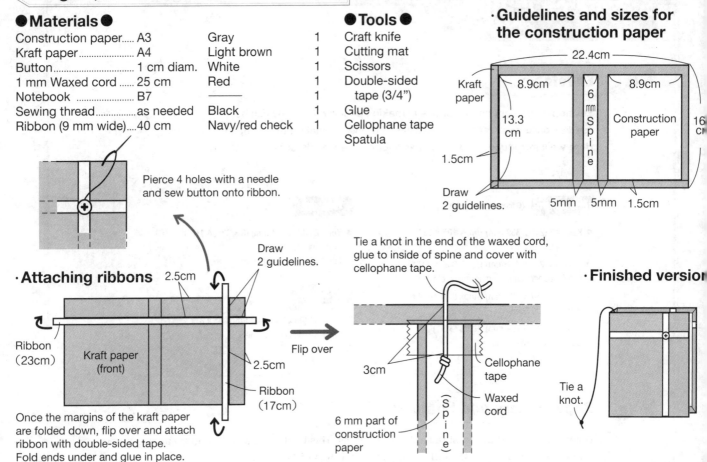

22.4cm

Kraft paper | 8.9cm | 6 mm Spine | 8.9cm
13.3 cm | Construction paper | 16 cm
1.5cm

Draw 2 guidelines.
5mm 5mm 1.5cm

Pierce 4 holes with a needle and sew button onto ribbon.

· Attaching ribbons

2.5cm

Draw 2 guidelines.

Ribbon (23cm)

Kraft paper (front)

Flip over

2.5cm

Ribbon (17cm)

Once the margins of the kraft paper are folded down, flip over and attach ribbon with double-sided tape.
Fold ends under and glue in place.

Tie a knot in the end of the waxed cord, glue to inside of spine and cover with cellophane tape.

3cm

6 mm part of construction paper

(Spine)

Cellophane tape

Waxed cord

· Finished version

Tie a knot.

Page 5, #3 Planner

● Materials ●

Construction paper.................	A3	Gray	1	
Wrapping paper........................	B5	Pastel check	1	
Contact paper	20 x 30 cm	———	1	
Planner	A6 size	———	1	
Clips	G clef shape	Pink gold	2	
Tyrolean tape (4 mm wide)...	20 cm	Pink floral	1	

● Tools ●

Double-sided tape (3/4")
Craft knife
Cutting mat
Scissors
Glue
Spatula

· Guidelines and sizes for the construction paper

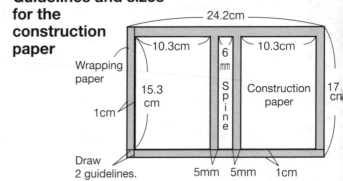

24.2cm

Wrapping paper | 10.3cm | 6 mm Spine | 10.3cm
15.3 cm | Construction paper | 17 cm
1cm

Draw 2 guidelines.
5mm 5mm 1cm

· Attaching contact paper

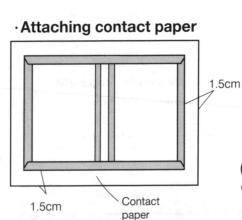

1.5cm

See p 31 for how to affix contact paper and add margins.

1.5cm

Contact paper

· Bookmark

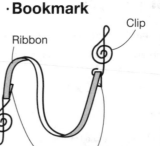

Ribbon

Clip

Glue ends.

· Finished version

Place clip.

schedule
1 2 3 4
5 6 7 8
9 10 11 12

Page 5, #4 Account Book with Folder

★See p 32 for instructions

Materials ●

Construction paper	A3	Gray	1
Wrapping paper	A3	Blue	1
Contact paper	35 x 45 cm	———	1
Clear folder	B5 size	Light blue	1
Account book	B5 size	———	1
Ribbon (5 mm wide)	36 cm	Yellow/red	1

Tools ●

Craft knife
Cutting mat
Scissors
Double-sided tape (3/4" and 1/4")
Glue
Spatula

· Guidelines and sizes for construction paper

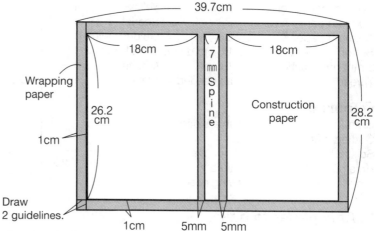

39.7cm
18cm
7 mm Spine
18cm
Wrapping paper
26.2 cm
1cm
Construction paper
28.2 cm
Draw 2 guidelines.
1cm   5mm   5mm

· Attaching contact paper

See p 31 for how to affix contact paper and add margins.

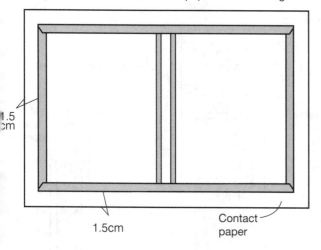

1.5 cm

1.5cm

Contact paper

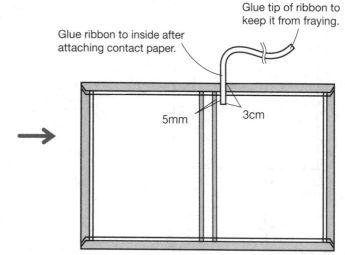

Glue tip of ribbon to keep it from fraying.

Glue ribbon to inside after attaching contact paper.

5mm   3cm

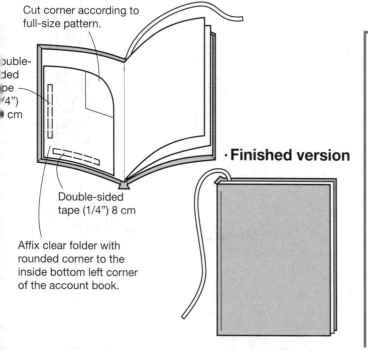

Cut corner according to full-size pattern.

Double-sided tape (1/4") 8 cm

Double-sided tape (1/4") 8 cm

Affix clear folder with rounded corner to the inside bottom left corner of the account book.

· Finished version

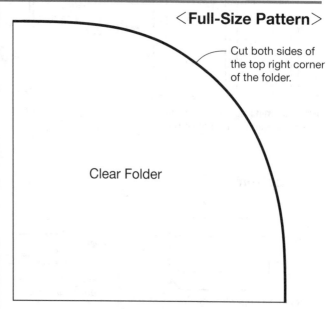

⟨**Full-Size Pattern**⟩

Cut both sides of the top right corner of the folder.

Clear Folder

35

Page 6, #5 Pen Case with Lid

●Materials●

Color construction paper..A3	Yellow	1
Textured paper A B3	Scarlet	1
Textured paper B B5	Golden yellow	1
Button .... 1.8 cm diam.	Olive brown	1
2 mm hair elastic .... 18 cm	Mocha	1
Thread .... as needed	Black	1

●Tools●

Craft knife	Double-sided tape (3/4")
Cutting mat	Glue
Scissors	Cellophane tape
Hole punch (2 mm)	Spatula
Wood mallet	Sewing needle

1. Make base.

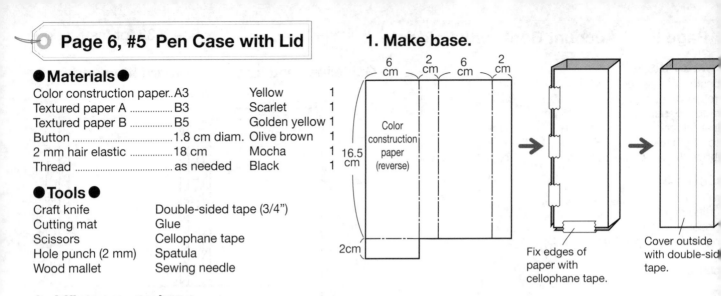

Color construction paper (reverse)

16.5 cm

2cm

Fix edges of paper with cellophane tape.

Cover outside with double-sided tape.

2. Affix paper to base.

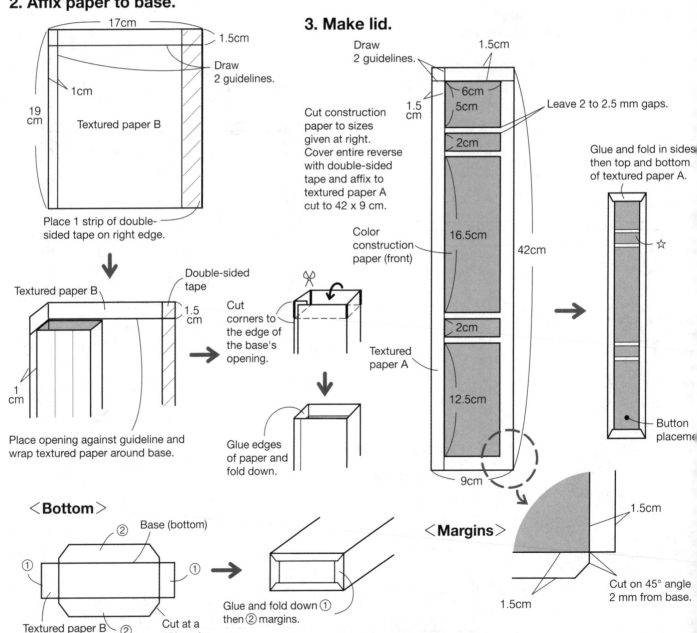

17cm

1.5cm

Draw 2 guidelines.

1cm

19 cm

Textured paper B

Place 1 strip of double-sided tape on right edge.

Textured paper B

Double-sided tape

1.5 cm

1 cm

Place opening against guideline and wrap textured paper around base.

Cut corners to the edge of the base's opening.

Glue edges of paper and fold down.

3. Make lid.

Draw 2 guidelines.

1.5cm

1.5 cm

6cm

5cm

2cm

Leave 2 to 2.5 mm gaps.

Cut construction paper to sizes given at right. Cover entire reverse with double-sided tape and affix to textured paper A cut to 42 x 9 cm.

Color construction paper (front)

16.5cm

42cm

Textured paper A

2cm

12.5cm

9cm

Glue and fold in sides then top and bottom of textured paper A.

☆

Button placement

<Bottom>

② Base (bottom)

① ①

Textured paper B ②

Cut at a 45° angle.

Glue and fold down ① then ② margins.

<Margins>

1.5cm

Cut on 45° angle 2 mm from base.

1.5cm

. Make reinforcement paper.

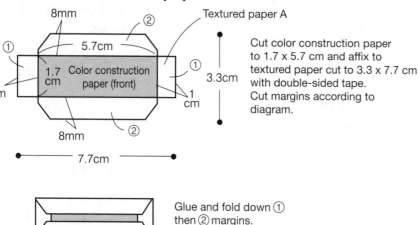

8mm
②
5.7cm
①
Textured paper A
1.7 cm Color construction paper (front)
①
1 cm
1 cm
8mm
②
3.3cm
7.7cm

Cut color construction paper to 1.7 x 5.7 cm and affix to textured paper cut to 3.3 x 7.7 cm with double-sided tape. Cut margins according to diagram.

Glue and fold down ① then ② margins.

5. Glue reinforcement paper to inside of lid.

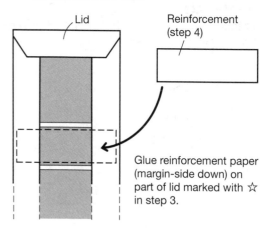

Lid

Reinforcement (step 4)

Glue reinforcement paper (margin-side down) on part of lid marked with ☆ in step 3.

. Make holes for the elastic.

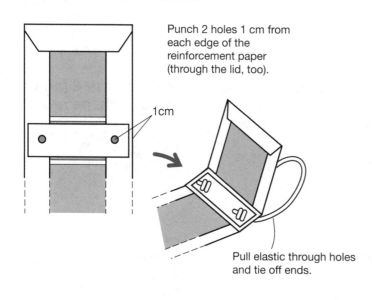

1cm

Punch 2 holes 1 cm from each edge of the reinforcement paper (through the lid, too).

Pull elastic through holes and tie off ends.

7. Add button.

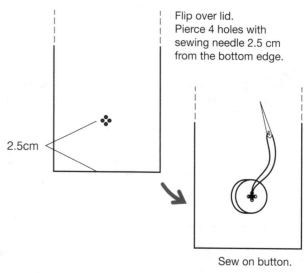

2.5cm

Flip over lid. Pierce 4 holes with sewing needle 2.5 cm from the bottom edge.

Sew on button.

8. Glue lid to base.

Lid

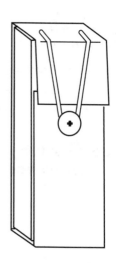

Base

Glue three sides.

9. Done!

●Materials●

Flat folder.................................B5E (appx 10 x 7")
Color construction paper....A3
Patterned paper....................12 x 12"

	#6	#7
	Pink	Light blue 1
	Pink	Light blue 1
	Peach dot	Aqua dot 1

●Tools●

Craft knife
Cutting mat
Scissors
Double-sided tape (3/4")
Glue
Cellophane tape
Spatula

3. Cut patterned paper.

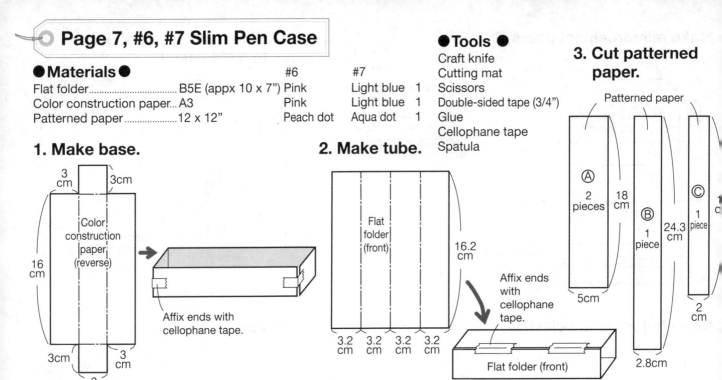

1. Make base.

3 cm / 3cm

Color construction paper (reverse)

16 cm

3cm / 3 cm

3 cm

Affix ends with cellophane tape.

2. Make tube.

Flat folder (front)

16.2 cm

Affix ends with cellophane tape.

3.2 cm 3.2 cm 3.2 cm 3.2 cm

Flat folder (front)

Patterned paper

Ⓐ 2 pieces 18 cm

Ⓑ 1 piece 24.3 cm

Ⓒ 1 piece

5cm

2 cm

2.8cm

4. Affix patterned paper Ⓐ to sides.

Cover reverse of patterned paper Ⓐ with double-sided tape and affix to side of base.

1cm 1cm
>1cm
>1cm
1cm

Repeat on opposite side with other sheet of patterned paper Ⓐ.
Cut paper at 4 top corners perpendicular to base. Cut on angles as in the diagram on the 4 bottom corners.

5. Glue and fold down edges of paper on the bottom (bottom view).

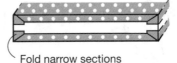

Fold narrow sections followed by long sections.

6. Glue and fold top sections down.

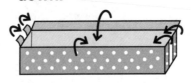

Draw guideline.

1cm

Patterned paper Ⓒ (cover reverse with double-sided tape).

Cut perpendicular lines at corners.

7. Fold patterned paper Ⓑ into a U-shape around ba

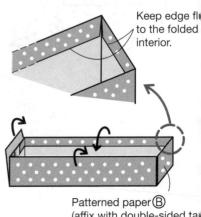

Keep edge fl to the folded interior.

Patterned paper Ⓑ (affix with double-sided ta

8. Cover seam of tube with patterned paper Ⓒ.

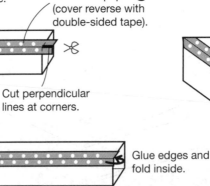

Glue edges and fold inside.

9. Done!

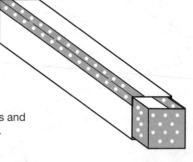

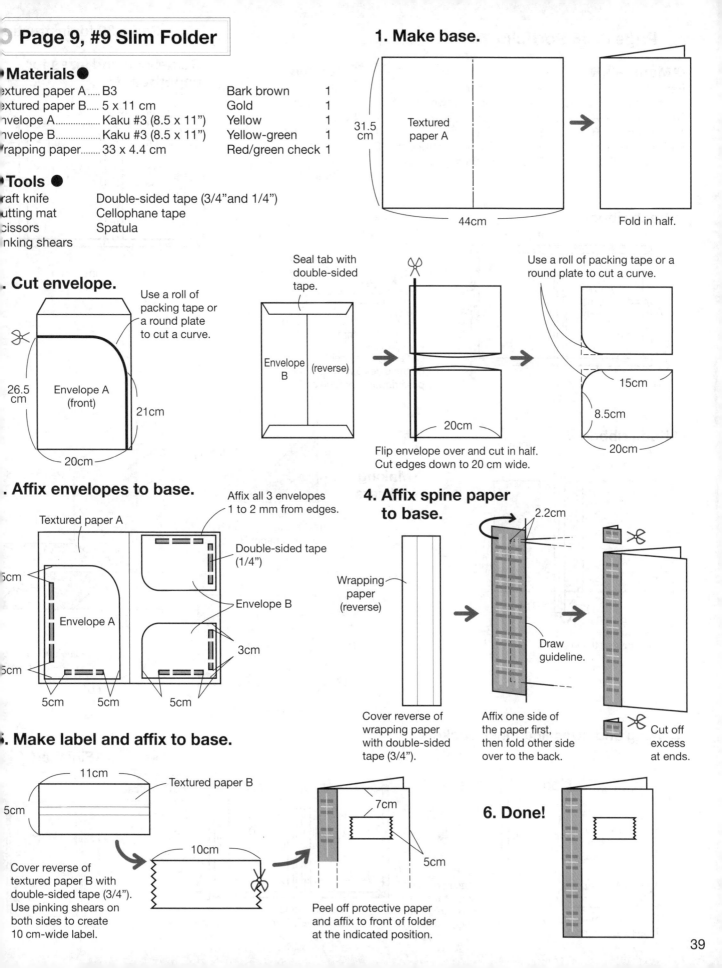

Page 9, #9 Slim Folder

● Materials ●

Textured paper A..... B3	Bark brown	1
Textured paper B..... 5 x 11 cm	Gold	1
Envelope A.................. Kaku #3 (8.5 x 11")	Yellow	1
Envelope B.................. Kaku #3 (8.5 x 11")	Yellow-green	1
Wrapping paper........ 33 x 4.4 cm	Red/green check	1

● Tools ●

Craft knife	Double-sided tape (3/4"and 1/4")
Cutting mat	Cellophane tape
Scissors	Spatula
Pinking shears	

1. Make base.

31.5 cm
Textured paper A
44cm
Fold in half.

2. Cut envelope.

Use a roll of packing tape or a round plate to cut a curve.

26.5 cm
Envelope A (front)
21cm
20cm

Seal tab with double-sided tape.

Envelope B (reverse)

Flip envelope over and cut in half.
Cut edges down to 20 cm wide.

Use a roll of packing tape or a round plate to cut a curve.

20cm
15cm
8.5cm
20cm

3. Affix envelopes to base.

Textured paper A

Affix all 3 envelopes 1 to 2 mm from edges.

Double-sided tape (1/4")

Envelope B

5cm
Envelope A
5cm

3cm

5cm 5cm 5cm

4. Affix spine paper to base.

2.2cm

Wrapping paper (reverse)

Cover reverse of wrapping paper with double-sided tape (3/4").

Draw guideline.

Affix one side of the paper first, then fold other side over to the back.

Cut off excess at ends.

5. Make label and affix to base.

11cm
Textured paper B
5cm

Cover reverse of textured paper B with double-sided tape (3/4").
Use pinking shears on both sides to create 10 cm-wide label.

10cm

7cm
5cm

Peel off protective paper and affix to front of folder at the indicated position.

6. Done!

Page 8, #8 Portfolio

● Materials ●

Paperboard	A3	White	1
Kraft paper	A3	Light brown	1
Textured paper A	B3	Lapis lazuli	2
Textured paper B	B5	Black	1
Ribbon A (6 mm wide)	37.5 cm	Black w/white dots	2
Ribbon B (2.5 cm wide)	37.5 cm	Red/black check	1

● Tools ●

Craft knife
Cutting mat
Scissors
Double-sided
  tape (3/4", 1/2")
Glue
Spatula

· Guidelines and sizes for paperboard

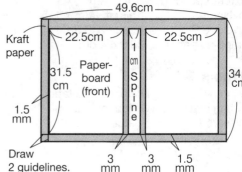

49.6cm

22.5cm | 1 cm Spine | 22.5cm

Kraft paper

31.5 cm — Paperboard (front)

34. cm

1.5 mm

Draw 2 guidelines.

3 mm   3 mm   1.5 mm

· Attach ribbon A

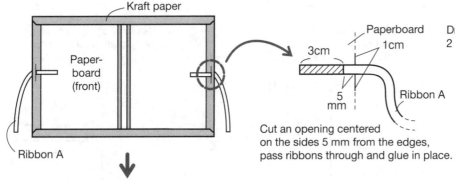

Kraft paper

Paper-board (front)

Ribbon A

Paperboard 1cm

3cm

5 mm

Ribbon A

Cut an opening centered on the sides 5 mm from the edges, pass ribbons through and glue in place.

· Attach ribbon B

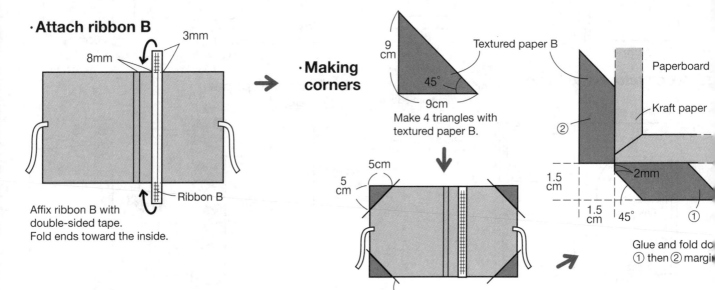

3mm

8mm

Ribbon B

Affix ribbon B with double-sided tape.
Fold ends toward the inside.

· Making corners

9 cm

45°

9cm

Textured paper B

Make 4 triangles with textured paper B.

5cm

5 cm

Draw guidelines.

Paperboard

Kraft paper

②

2mm

1.5 cm

1.5 cm   45°

①

Glue and fold do
① then ② margin

· Making and attaching inner pockets

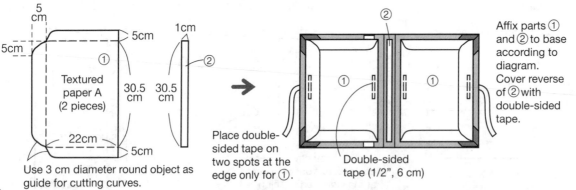

5 cm

5cm

5cm

①

Textured paper A (2 pieces)

30.5 cm

22cm

5cm

Use 3 cm diameter round object as guide for cutting curves.

1cm

30.5 cm

②

Place double-sided tape on two spots at the edge only for ①.

②

①

①

Double-sided tape (1/2", 6 cm)

Affix parts ① and ② to base according to diagram. Cover reverse of ② with double-sided tape.

· Finished version

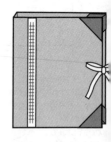

Materials ●

	#15	#16	#17	
Construction paper..........A3	Gray	Gray	Gray	1
Textured paper...................B5	Fresh green	Fuscia	Sky blue	1
Decorative twist tie ....☆	Yellow/white dots	Blue/white dots	Red/white dots	1
Clips..	Pink gold (flower)	Silver (fish)	Gold (star)	1

☆ Cut twist ties to 10 cm for #15, 7 cm for #16 and 13 cm for #17

● Tools ●

Craft knife
Cutting mat
Double-sided tape (3/4")
Cellophane tape
Glue

1. Make base.
Make 2 of each base from construction paper according to the diagrams below. Remove gray sections.

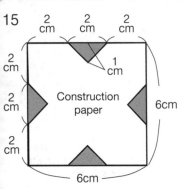

15

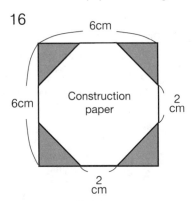

16

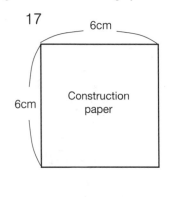

17

2. Affix base to textured paper.

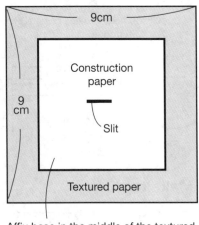

Affix base in the middle of the textured paper with double-sided tape.
Cut a 1 cm slit in the middle.

3. Attach clip with twist tie.

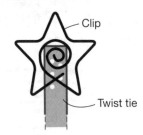

Clip
Twist tie

Affix the back of the clip only to the tie with cellophane tape. Fold the tape over towards the back of the tie.

4. Insert twist tie into base and cover with other base paper.

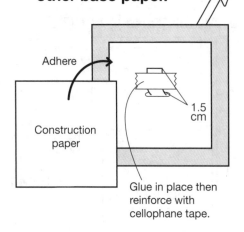

Adhere

Construction paper

1.5 cm

Glue in place then reinforce with cellophane tape.

5. Fold textured paper under.
Remove gray sections. Glue down ① parts followed by ② parts.

15

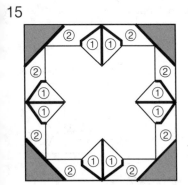

16

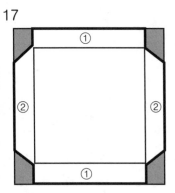

17

6. Done!

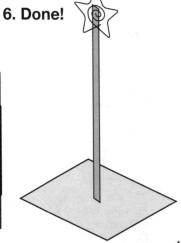

<Instructions for #10>

● #10 Materials ●

Flat folder	A4E size	Pink	1
Envelope	Kaku #3 (8.5 x 11")	Pink	8
Brads	8 mm diam.	Pink gold	4
Ribbon (3 mm wide)	30 cm	Orange/white	1

● #11 Materials ●

Flat folder	B5E size	Cream	1
Envelope	Kaku #2 (9 x 13")	Cream	1
Brads	8 mm diam.	Silver	2
Ribbon A (3 mm wide)	30 cm	Pink/white	1
Ribbon B (1 cm wide)	50 cm	Pink/light pink	1

● #12 Materials ●

Flat folder	B5E size	Green	1
Envelope	You #2 (C6)	Cream	7
Brads	8 mm diam.	Gold	2
Ribbon (3 mm wide)	30 cm	Blue/white	1

● Tools ●

Craft knife
Cutting mat
Scissors
Double-sided tape (3/4")
2 mm hole punch
Wood mallet
Cylindrical pencil
Spatula

1. Remove clip and staples from flat folder.

Flat folder (reverse, unlined side)

★ In the finished product, the reverse ends up on the outside.

Flip Ⓠ

Ⓠ (reverse)

Ⓐ

2. Open flat folder, cut and fold according to diagram.

Flat file (front, lined side)

①
②

2cm
3.5cm

15.5 cm

Preexisting fold lines

Middle (Longer side on the bottom)

15.5 cm

Preexisting fold lines

2cm
1.5cm
1cm
1cm

Ⓐ
Ⓑ
Ⓒ
Ⓓ

6cm

Ⓔ 4cm

Flip Ⓩ

Ⓠ

Affix part Ⓐ on the center of the fold line of part Ⓠ with double-sided tape.

Ⓩ

Affix part Ⓒ on top of topmost fold line of part Ⓩ with double-sided tape.

Ⓒ

Ⓩ (reverse)

3. Attach parts Ⓠ and Ⓩ.

Ⓩ (front)

①
②

Ⓠ (front)

Place double-sided tape on section ① of part Ⓠ and attach to part Ⓩ. Place a ruler next to both pieces to ensure evenness.

5. Make and attach handle.

4cm   4cm

1 1   1 1
cm cm Ⓑ (reverse) cm cm

5 mm marks

Curve center with cylindrical pencil.

2.5 cm

Attach handle with double-sided tape. Cut along marks, insert brads and spread on the inside.

Ⓐ

Ⓠ (reverse)

6. Make tag.

Cut curves into the 3 pointed corners to match original curved corner from folder. Punch a hole in one end, loop ribbon through hole and knot.

Ribbo[n]

4. Fold up bag.

Don't fold here.

Ⓩ (reverse)

Ⓠ (front)

② ①

Fold preexisting fold lines of part Ⓩ. Don't fold the bottom fold line.

Affix part Ⓓ with double sided tape, hiding the ends of the brads.

Ⓩ (front)

Ⓓ

. Cut envelopes.

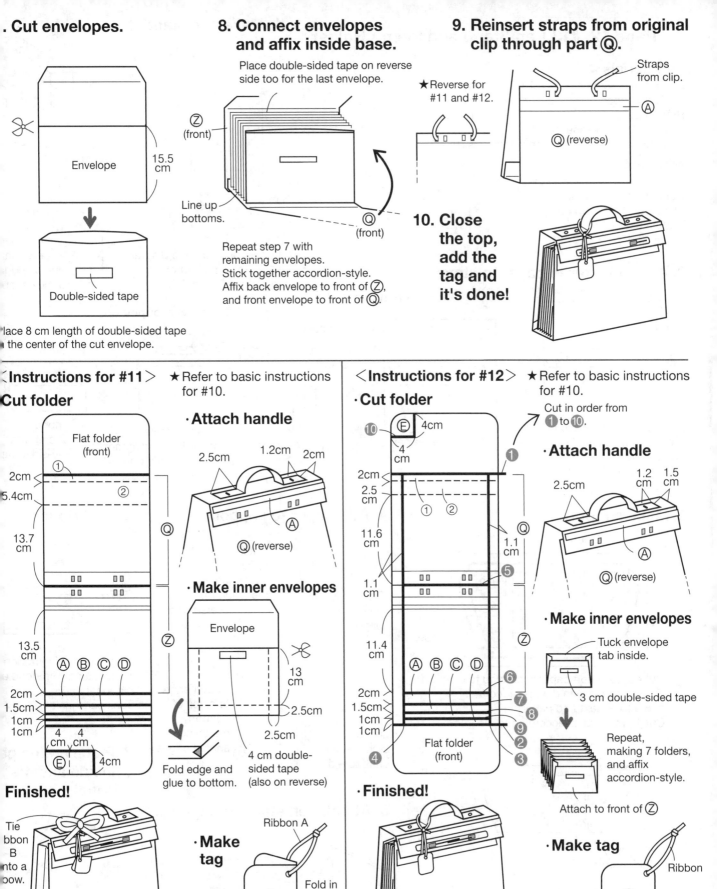

Envelope
15.5 cm

✂

Double-sided tape

Place 8 cm length of double-sided tape in the center of the cut envelope.

8. Connect envelopes and affix inside base.

Place double-sided tape on reverse side too for the last envelope.

Ⓩ (front)

Line up bottoms.

Ⓠ (front)

Repeat step 7 with remaining envelopes. Stick together accordion-style. Affix back envelope to front of Ⓩ, and front envelope to front of Ⓠ.

9. Reinsert straps from original clip through part Ⓠ.

★ Reverse for #11 and #12.

Straps from clip.

Ⓐ

Ⓠ (reverse)

10. Close the top, add the tag and it's done!

‹Instructions for #11›
★ Refer to basic instructions for #10.

·Cut folder

Flat folder (front)

① 2cm
5.4cm ②

13.7 cm

Ⓠ

13.5 cm

Ⓩ

Ⓐ Ⓑ Ⓒ Ⓓ

2cm
1.5cm
1cm
1cm

4 cm   4 cm

Ⓔ   4cm

·Attach handle

2.5cm 1.2cm 2cm

Ⓐ

Ⓠ (reverse)

·Make inner envelopes

Envelope ✂

13 cm

2.5cm

4 cm double-sided tape (also on reverse)

Fold edge and glue to bottom.

·Finished!

Tie ribbon B into a bow.

·Make tag

Ribbon A

Round corners   Ⓔ   Fold in half.

‹Instructions for #12›
★ Refer to basic instructions for #10.

·Cut folder

Cut in order from ① to ⑩.

⑩ Ⓔ 4cm
4 cm
①

2cm
2.5 cm

11.6 cm   ① ②

Ⓠ   1.1 cm

1.1 cm   ⑤

Ⓩ

11.4 cm

Ⓐ Ⓑ Ⓒ Ⓓ

2cm
1.5cm
1cm
1cm

Flat folder (front)

⑥ ⑦ ⑧ ⑨ ② ③
④

·Attach handle

2.5cm   1.2 cm   1.5 cm

Ⓐ

Ⓠ (reverse)

·Make inner envelopes

Tuck envelope tab inside.

3 cm double-sided tape

Repeat, making 7 folders, and affix accordion-style.

Attach to front of Ⓩ

·Finished!

·Make tag

Ribbon

Round corners   Ⓔ

● Materials ●

Construction paper	A3 Gray	1
Textured paper	A4 Gray	2
Ribbon	☆ Pink/black	1
Memo pad (store-bought)		1

☆ Ribbon width is 1 cm. The length is (a+b) x 2 plus 8 cm.

● Tools ●

Craft knife	Cellophane tape
Cutting mat	Glue
Scissors	Spatula
Double-sided tape (3/4")	

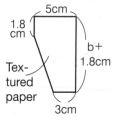
— Memo pad size —
Length = b
Width = a

1. Make pen stand.

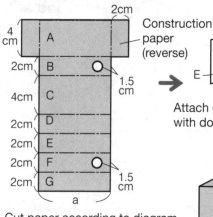

2cm
4 cm — A
2cm — B ○ — 1.5 cm
4cm — C
2cm — D
2cm — E
2cm — F ○ — 1.5 cm
2cm — G
a

Construction paper (reverse)

Cut paper according to diagram.
Cut 1.2 cm diameter holes with knife in parts B and F.

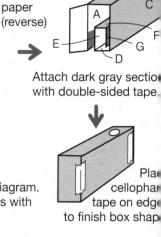

Attach dark gray section with double-sided tape.

Place cellophane tape on edge to finish box shape.

2. Attach textured paper to stand.

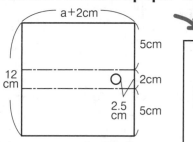

a+2cm
5cm
12 cm — ○ — 2cm
2.5 cm — 5cm

Cut paper according to diagram and cover with double-sided tape. Cut a 1.2 cm diameter hole with knife in the middle, 2.5 cm from the right edge.

< View from above >

Textured paper
Part B of box from step 1

B

Align holes in part B and textured paper.

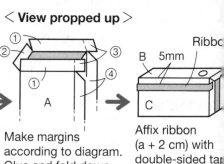

Wrap paper around box.

Make margins according to diagram. Glue and fold down in numbered order.

Affix ribbon (a + 2 cm) with double-sided tape.

B 5mm Ribbon
C

3. Make support.

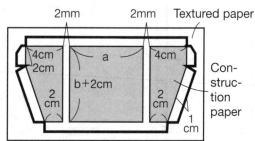

2mm 2mm Textured paper
4cm a 4cm
2cm b+2cm 2cm — Construction paper
2 cm 2 cm
1 cm

Cut construction paper according to diagram. Cover reverse with double-sided tape and affix to textured paper. Cut 1 cm margins according to diagram.

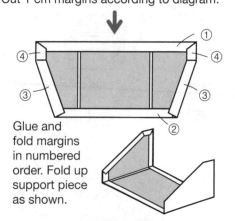

Glue and fold margins in numbered order. Fold up support piece as shown.

4. Add paper to support.

5cm
1.8 cm
Tex-tured paper — b+ 1.8cm
3cm

Cut 2 pieces of textured paper according to the diagram. Cover reverse with double-sided tape.

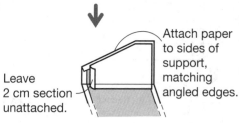

Leave 2 cm section unattached.

Attach paper to sides of support, matching angled edges.

5. Attach pen stand to support.

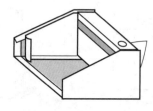

Align back of pen stand with vertical edges of support and glue together on the sides and bottom.

6. Add ribbon.

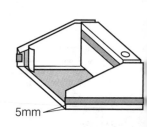

5mm

Attach remaining ribbon to the stand with double-sided tape.
Tuck ends inside.

7. Place memo pad inside and it's done!

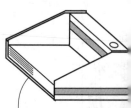

Attach base of pad to stand with double-sided tape.

Page 15, #18, #19 Clip Box

Materials ●

Color construction paper.. A3
Textured paper A B5
Textured paper B B5
Textured paper C B5
Magnetic sheet 3.9 x 3.9 cm

	#18	#19	
	Yellow-green	Yellow	1
	Sunflower	Sky blue	1
	Sky blue	Fuscia	1
	Fuscia	Fresh green	1
	(n/a)	Yellow-green	1

Tools ●

Craft knife   Glue
Cutting mat   Spatula
Double-sided
tape (3/4")
Cellophane tape

─── Legend ───
Where there are 2 measurements
listed, the top is for #18 and the
bottom is #19. If there's only
1 measurement it applies to both.

1. Make base.

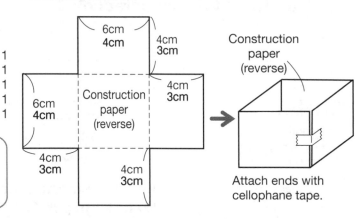

6cm 4cm   4cm 3cm
6cm 4cm   Construction paper (reverse)   4cm 3cm
4cm 3cm   4cm 3cm

Construction paper (reverse)

Attach ends with cellophane tape.

2. Attach textured paper to base.

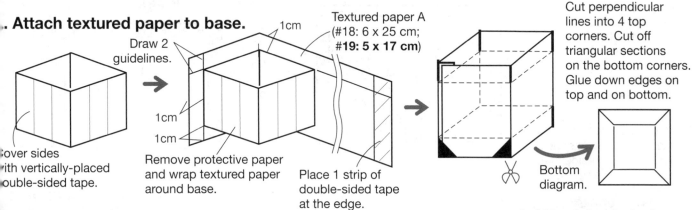

Draw 2 guidelines.   1cm

Textured paper A
(#18: 6 x 25 cm;
#19: 5 x 17 cm)

1cm
1cm

Cut perpendicular lines into 4 top corners. Cut off triangular sections on the bottom corners. Glue down edges on top and on bottom.

Cover sides with vertically-placed double-sided tape.

Remove protective paper and wrap textured paper around base.

Place 1 strip of double-sided tape at the edge.

Bottom diagram.

3. Make lid and bottom.

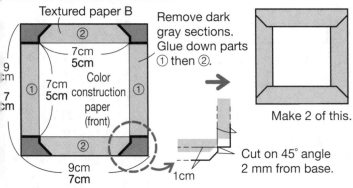

Textured paper B

②
7cm 5cm
9cm ① 7cm 5cm Color construction paper (front) ①
7cm
②
9cm 7cm

Remove dark gray sections. Glue down parts ① then ②.

1cm

Cut on 45° angle 2 mm from base.

Make 2 of this.

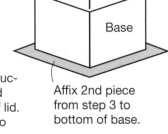

18: Color construction paper
19: Magnetic sheet

#18: Cut 2 pieces of construction paper 5.9 x 5.9 cm and attach both to underside of lid.
#19: Glue magnetic sheet to underside of lid.

4. Attach body to base.

Base

Affix 2nd piece from step 3 to bottom of base.

5. Make lid decoration.

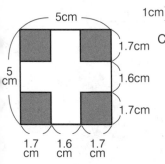

5cm
5cm   1.7cm
                  1.6cm
                  1.7cm
1.7cm 1.6cm 1.7cm
cm   cm   cm

#18: Cut textured paper C according to pattern at far right.
#19: Cut textured paper C according to above diagram.

6. Make handle.

38cm
1cm

Color construction paper (front)

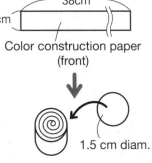

1.5 cm diam.

Glue reverse side of construction paper and coil tightly. Glue round piece of paper on top.

7. Attach handle and decoration and it's done!

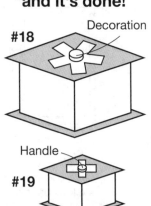

Decoration

#18

Handle

#19

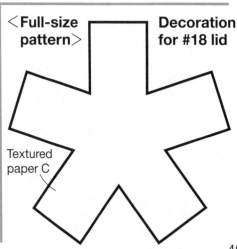

＜Full-size pattern＞   Decoration for #18 lid

Textured paper C

1. Cut color construction paper.

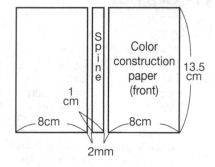

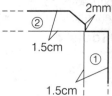

Cut corners of margin parts ②, then glue and fold down ① then ② margins.

● Materials ●

Color construction paper.... A3	Yellow-green	1
Textured paper A A4	Peach	1
Textured paper B B5	Light brown	1
Textured paper C B5	Bark brown	1
Ribbon (1 cm wide) .... 20 cm	Brown/white	2
Sticky notes A .... 7.5 x 12.7 cm	Yellow	1
Sticky notes B .... 7.5 x 7.5 cm	Light blue	1
Sticky notes C .... 3.7 x 5 cm	1 each pink, cream	

● Tools ●

Craft knife
Cutting mat
Scissors
Double-sided tape (3/4")
Cellophane tape
Glue
Cylindrical pencil
Spatula

Textured paper A
(Cover reverse of construction paper with double-sided tape and attach to textured paper.)

2. Affix construction paper to textured paper A.

Draw 2 guidelines.

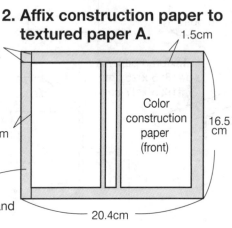

3. Glue and fold in edges.

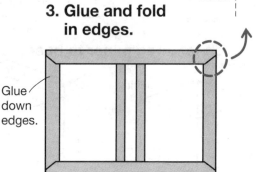

Glue down edges.

4. Make belt and loop.

< **Belt** >

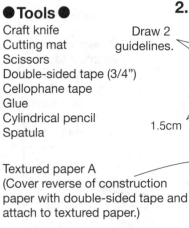

Glue both pieces together. Curve end with pencil before glue sets.

< **Loop** >

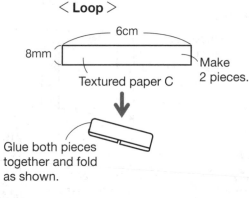

6cm
8mm
Textured paper C
Make 2 pieces.

Glue both pieces together and fold as shown.

5. Add ribbon to base.

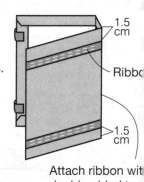

1.5 cm

Ribbon

1.5 cm

Attach ribbon with double-sided tape with base folded closed.

6. Glue belt and loop to base.

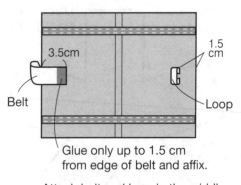

3.5cm
1.5 cm
Belt
Loop

Glue only up to 1.5 cm from edge of belt and affix.

Attach belt and loop in the middle on each side.

7. Affix sticky notes to inside of base.

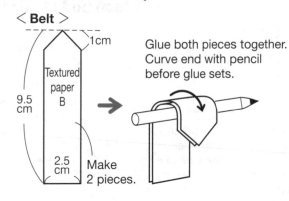

Sticky notes B

Sticky notes A

Sticky notes C

Attach double-stick tape to the back of each pack of notes and stick to base according to diagram.

8. Done!

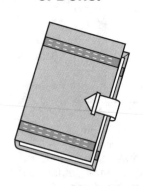

Materials ●

	#20	#21	
osterboard A3	White/gray	White/gray	1
atterned paper.........30.5 x 30.5 cm	Mint dot	Strawberry dot	1
xtured paper............A4	Bark brown	Bark brown	1
mm hair elastic ....5 cm	Brown	Brown	1
hell button ....1.3 cm diam.	White	White	1
hread ....as needed	White	White	1

● Tools ●

Craft knife
Cutting mat
Scissors
Double-sided tape (3/4")
Cellophane tape
Glue
Spatula
Sewing needle

Instructions for #20 > ☆Patterned paper and textured paper are reversed for #21.

1. Make base.

8cm   8cm   8cm

Poster-board (front)

Reserve all removed corners.

osterboard (ront)

Attach ends with cellophane tape.

2. Cover base with patterned paper.

Cover 3 sides and diagonally striped sections on 4th side with double-sided tape.

1.5 cm   1.5 cm

Draw 2 guidelines.

1.5cm

(Reverse)

1.5cm

1.5cm

Peel off protective tape and affix paper.

#20: Patterned paper
#21: Textured paper
(11 x 27 cm)

Cut perpendicular lines into all 8 corners. Glue and fold down margins on top and bottom.

#20: Patterned paper
#21: Textured paper
(3 x 7.8 cm, folded)

Affix paper to front edge of opening.

< View of bottom >

3. Attach button.

Side without paper.

1.5 cm

Pierce two holes 1.5 cm from top with sewing needle.

Sew on button.

Turn 180°

Cut a 3 x 3 cm piece of paper and cover ends of thread.

4. Make lid.

Draw 2 guidelines.

#20: Textured paper
#21: Patterned paper

1.5cm

1.5cm

27.6cm

②

Poster-board (front)

11 cm   ①

①

②

3 mm   3 mm

Use 3 of the 4 corners cut in step 1.

Glue and fold down ① then ② margins.

1.5cm

1.5cm

Cut on an angle 2 mm from the inner edge.

Cut a 7.8 x 3 cm piece of paper and affix over right-hand seam.

Loop and glue elastic then reinforce with cellophane tape.

Continued on p 48

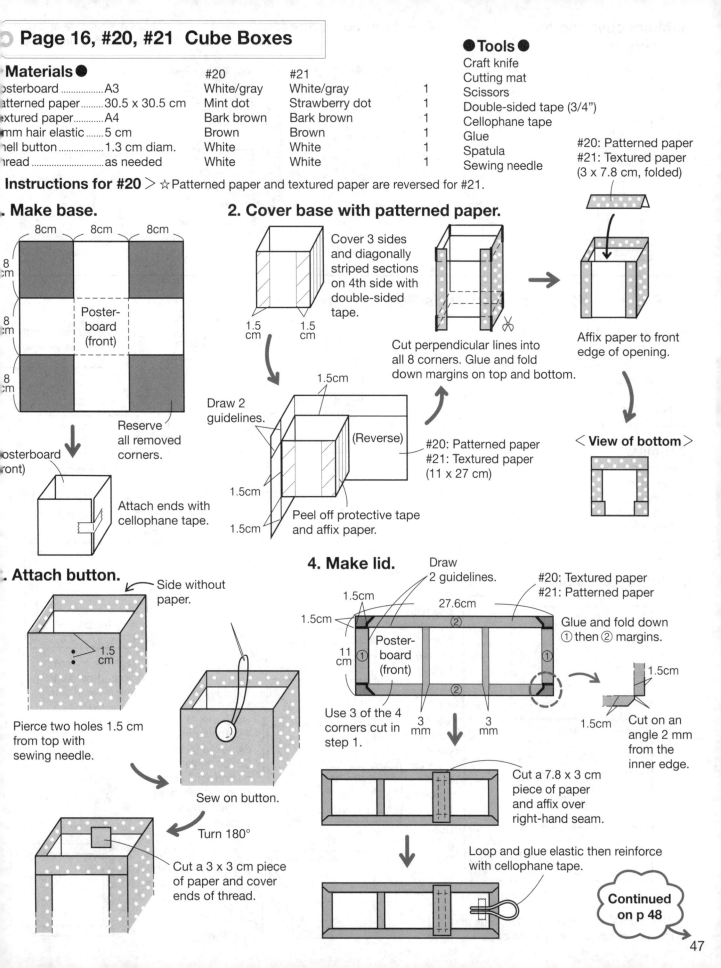

5. Make covering for inside of lid.

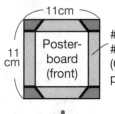

11cm

11 cm

Poster-board (front)

#20: Textured paper
#21: Patterned paper
(Cut off dark gray parts.)

Glue and fold margins

6. Attach lid to base.

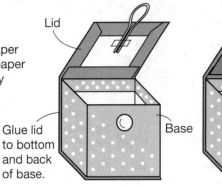

Lid

Glue lid to bottom and back of base.

Base

Glue margin side of covering from step 5 to underside of l

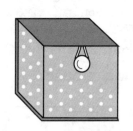

7. Done!

Page 17, #22 Odds-and-Ends Box

Page 17, #22 Odds-and-Ends Box

● Materials ●

Construction paper.................A3	Gray	1
Color construction paper.....A3	Pink	1
Textured paper A....................B4	Apricot	1
Textured paper B....................B4	Gold	1
Ribbon A (1cm wide)..............22 cm	Orange	3
Ribbon B (1cm wide)..............7 cm	Orange	1

● Tools ●

Craft knife
Cutting board
Scissors
Double-sided tape (1/2")
Cellophane tape
Glue
Spatula

1. Make box.

16.5cm
5cm
5cm
12.5 cm

Color construction paper (reverse)

5cm
5cm

Attach ends with cellophane tape

Construction paper (revers

4. Make covering for inside of lid.

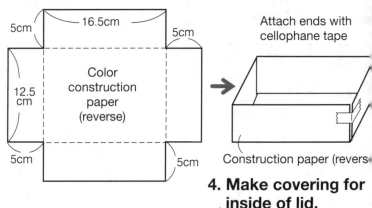

Ⓐ
②
12.2 cm
Construction paper
①
①
16.2cm
②

Cut paper to size indicated by diagram, cover reverse with double-sided tape and stick to part Ⓐ.

Cut on a angle 2 from the inner edg

1.5cm

Glue and fold down ① then ② margins.

3. Attach parts Ⓑ and Ⓒ of textured paper B to box.

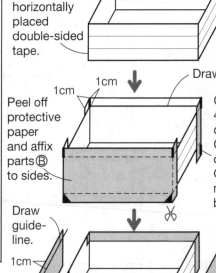

Cover sides of box with horizontally placed double-sided tape.

1cm
1cm

Peel off protective paper and affix parts Ⓑ to sides.

Draw guideline.

Draw guide-line.

1cm

Draw guideline.

Cut paper at top 4 corners perpendicular to base. Cut on angles on bottom 4 corners. Glue and fold down margins on top and bottom.

Glue both edges.

2. Cut textured paper B.

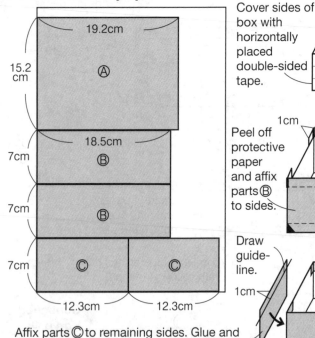

19.2cm
15.2 cm
Ⓐ

18.5cm
7cm
Ⓑ

7cm
Ⓑ

7cm
Ⓒ
Ⓒ

12.3cm
12.3cm

Affix parts Ⓒ to remaining sides. Glue and fold down margins on top and bottom.

48

Make lid.

Cover reverse of construction paper with double-sided tape and stick to textured paper A. Glue and fold parts ① then ② of the margin.

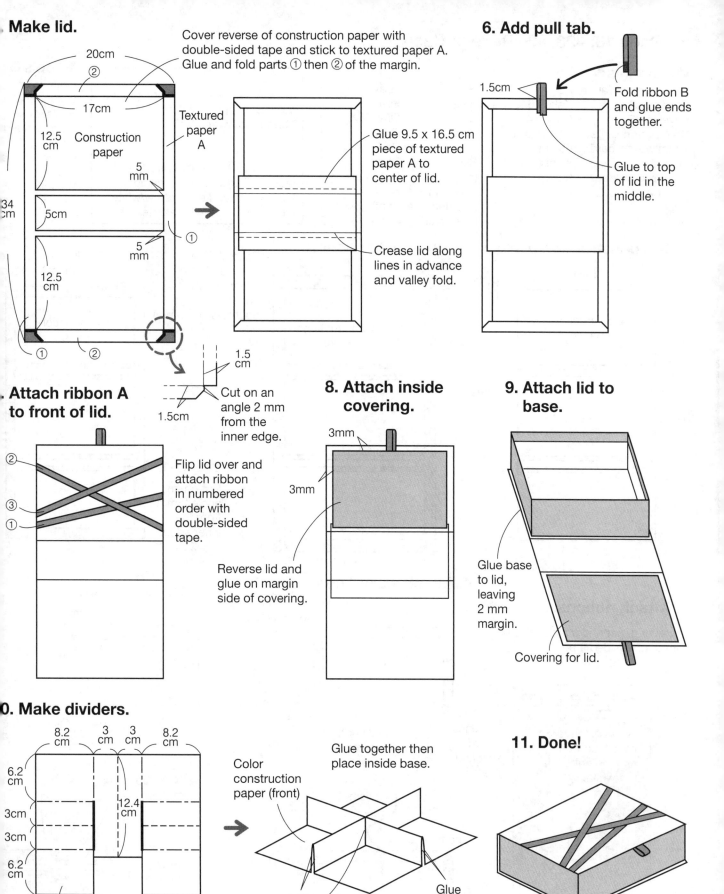

20cm

②

17cm

Textured paper A

12.5 cm Construction paper

5 mm

34 cm

5cm

5 mm

①

12.5 cm

① ②

Glue 9.5 x 16.5 cm piece of textured paper A to center of lid.

Crease lid along lines in advance and valley fold.

6. Add pull tab.

1.5cm

Fold ribbon B and glue ends together.

Glue to top of lid in the middle.

1.5 cm

Cut on an angle 2 mm from the inner edge.

1.5cm

Attach ribbon A to front of lid.

②

③

①

Flip lid over and attach ribbon in numbered order with double-sided tape.

8. Attach inside covering.

3mm

3mm

Reverse lid and glue on margin side of covering.

9. Attach lid to base.

Glue base to lid, leaving 2 mm margin.

Covering for lid.

0. Make dividers.

8.2 cm   3 cm   3 cm   8.2 cm

6.2 cm

3cm

3cm

6.2 cm

12.4 cm

Copy above pattern onto color construction paper (reverse) and fold.

Color construction paper (front)

Glue together then place inside base.

Glue here.

Glue here.

11. Done!

Page 18, #23, #24 Receipt Case

● Materials ●

		#23	#24	
Construction paper	A3	Gray	Gray	1
Envelope A	Kaku #6 (C5)	Beige	(n/a)	4
Envelope B	Chou #4 (4 x 8")	Gray	Gray	3
Shell button	2.2 cm diam.	Gray	Gray	1
1 mm waxed cord	60 cm	Olive brown	Red	1
Thread	as needed	Black	Black	1
Air mail envelope	9.2 x 16.5 cm	(n/a)	Light blue	8
Paper A	B4	(see details at right)		1
Paper B	B4	(see details at right)		1
Ribbon (7 mm wide)	25 cm	(see details at right)		2

#23
Paper A: Waterproof wrapping paper
Paper B: Wrapping paper (letter motif)
Ribbon: Navy/red check

#24
Paper A: Textured paper (red)
Paper B: Textured paper (indigo)
Ribbon: 1 strand each red w/white dots, navy blue w/white dots

● Tools ●
Craft knife
Cutting mat
Scissors
Double-sided tape (3/4")
Cellophane ta
Glue
Spatula
Sewing needl

1. Cut construction paper.

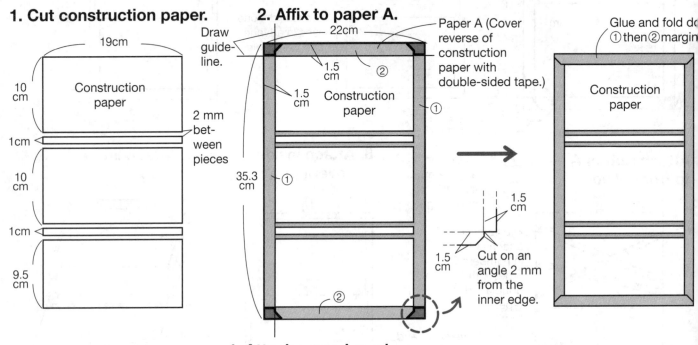

19cm
10 cm — Construction paper
2 mm between pieces
1cm
10 cm
1cm
9.5 cm

2. Affix to paper A.

Draw guide-line.
22cm
Paper A (Cover reverse of construction paper with double-sided tape.)
1.5 cm ②
1.5 cm — Construction paper
①
35.3 cm ①
②

1.5 cm
1.5 cm
Cut on an angle 2 mm from the inner edge.

Glue and fold do
① then ② margin
Construction paper

3. Attach ribbons.

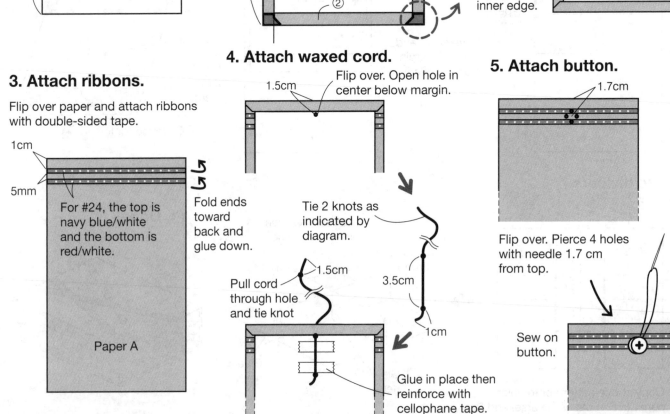

Flip over paper and attach ribbons with double-sided tape.

1cm
5mm
For #24, the top is navy blue/white and the bottom is red/white.
Paper A

4. Attach waxed cord.

1.5cm
Flip over. Open hole in center below margin.

Fold ends toward back and glue down.

Tie 2 knots as indicated by diagram.

1.5cm
Pull cord through hole and tie knot

3.5cm

1cm

Glue in place then reinforce with cellophane tape.

5. Attach button.

1.7cm

Flip over. Pierce 4 holes with needle 1.7 cm from top.

Sew on button.

Affix paper B to reverse.

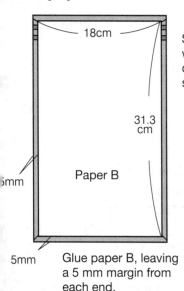

18cm

31.3 cm

5mm

Paper B

5mm

Glue paper B, leaving a 5 mm margin from each end.

Cut envelope B.

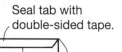

Seal tab with double-sided tape.

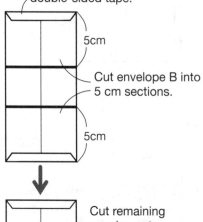

5cm

Cut envelope B into 5 cm sections.

5cm

Cut remaining envelopes to make 6 dividers.

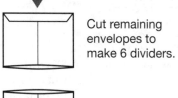

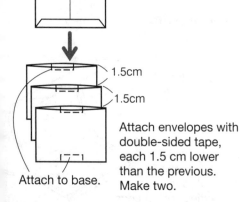

1.5cm

1.5cm

Attach envelopes with double-sided tape, each 1.5 cm lower than the previous. Make two.

Attach to base.

7. Cut envelope A (#23 only).

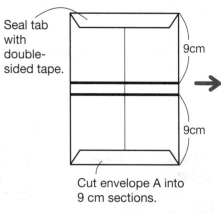

Seal tab with double-sided tape.

9cm

9cm

Cut envelope A into 9 cm sections.

Cut remaining envelopes to make 8 dividers.

Line up dividers and attach accordion-style with 6 cm lengths of double-sided tape placed in the center. Add double-sided tape on reverse side too for the last divider.

(#24 only)

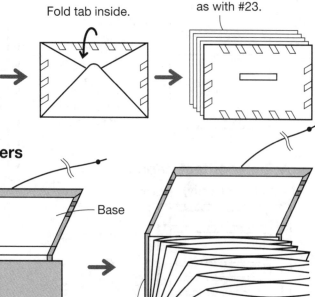

Air mail

Fold tab inside.

Attach accordion-style as with #23.

9. Attach dividers to base.

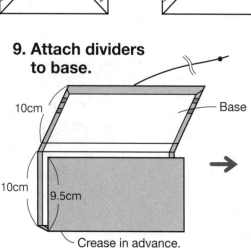

10cm

Base

10cm

9.5cm

Crease in advance.

Attach front and back of dividers to inside of base with double-sided tape.

10. Attach envelopes from step 8.

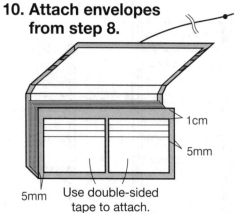

1cm

5mm

5mm

Use double-sided tape to attach.

11. Done!

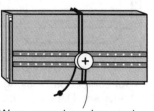

Wrap waxed cord around button to close.

51

Page 19, #25, #26, #27 Card Case

● Materials ●

Color construction paper..	A3	Pink	Yellow	Black	1
Outside paper	B5	Brown	Yellow/light yellow dots	Black/white dots	1
Card envelopes	6.5 x 10.2 cm	Light pink	Yellow-green	Light blue	10
Contact paper	30 x 20 cm	(n/a)	——	——	1
2 mm hair elastic	20 cm	Mocha	Patterned orange	Dark red	1
Thread	as neeeded	Black	Black	Black	1
Shell button		White (2 cm)	Gray (2.3 cm)	Gray (1.8 cm)	1

● Tools ●

Craft knife
Cutting mat
Scissors
Double-sided tape (3
Glue
2 mm hole punch
Wood mallet
Spatula
Sewing needle

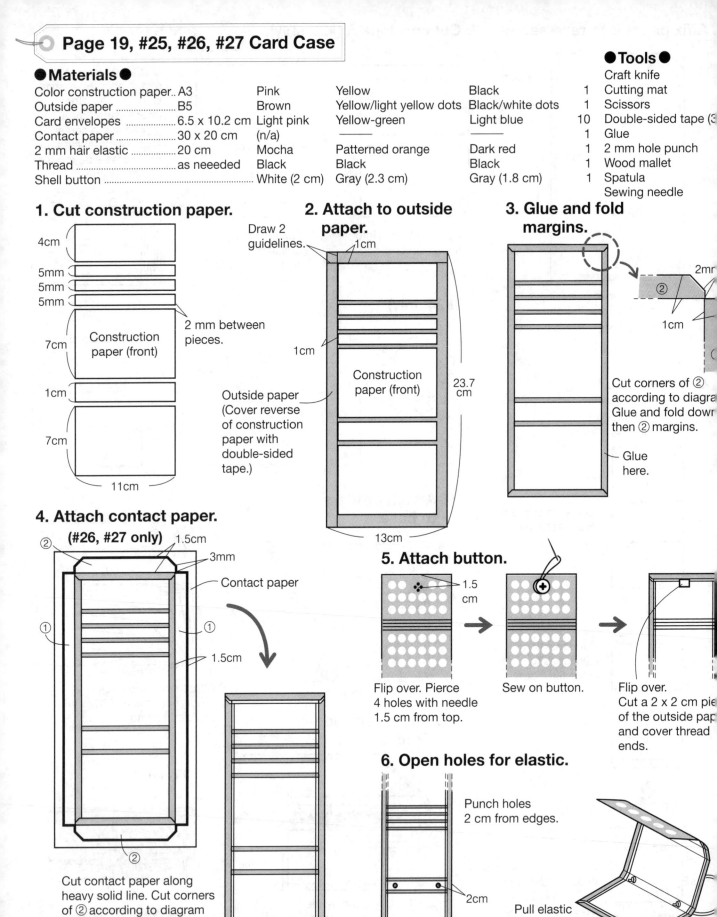

1. Cut construction paper.

4cm

5mm
5mm
5mm

2 mm between pieces.

7cm — Construction paper (front)

1cm

7cm

11cm

2. Attach to outside paper.

Draw 2 guidelines.

1cm

1cm

Construction paper (front)

23.7 cm

Outside paper (Cover reverse of construction paper with double-sided tape.)

13cm

3. Glue and fold margins.

2mr

②

1cm

Cut corners of ② according to diagra Glue and fold dowr then ② margins.

Glue here.

4. Attach contact paper.

(#26, #27 only)

1.5cm

3mm

Contact paper

②

①

①

1.5cm

②

Cut contact paper along heavy solid line. Cut corners of ② according to diagram and fold edges ① then ②.

5. Attach button.

1.5 cm

Flip over. Pierce 4 holes with needle 1.5 cm from top.

Sew on button.

Flip over. Cut a 2 x 2 cm pie of the outside pap and cover thread ends.

6. Open holes for elastic.

Punch holes 2 cm from edges.

2cm

Pull elastic through and tie knots in ends.

Connect card envelopes.

card envelope

Fold tab inside.

lace 4 to 5 cm strip double-sided tape center of envelope.

Double-sided tape

dd double-sided pe on reverse side o for the last nvelope.

Repeat with other envelopes and attach accordion-style.

8. Add dividers to base.

Attach 1 to 2 mm from inside top edge.

After attaching back envelope, peel off protective paper from front piece of double-sided tape and fold up front of base.

9. Done!

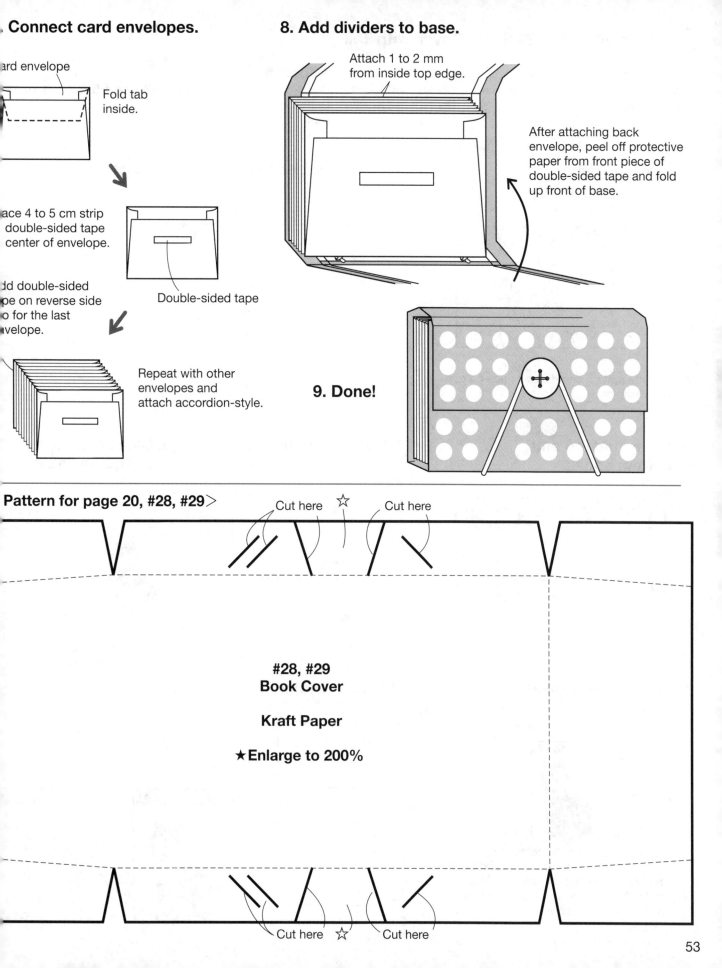

Pattern for page 20, #28, #29 ＞

Cut here ☆ Cut here

#28, #29
Book Cover

Kraft Paper

★**Enlarge to 200%**

Cut here ☆ Cut here

● Materials ●

	#28	#29	
Kraft paper...............A3	Light brown	Light brown	1
Textured paper.......B5	Black	Gold	1
Clear folder.............B5	Brown	Orange	1

● Tools ●

Craft knife
Cutting mat
Glue

☆ **See p 53 and 55 for patterns**

1. Cut kraft paper.

Make 6 incisions.

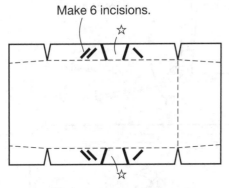

Enlarge pattern on p 53 and trace pattern onto kraft paper.

2. Glue and fold down ☆ sections.

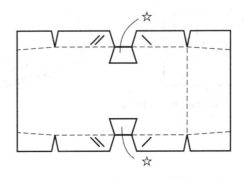

3. Valley fold top and bottom edges.

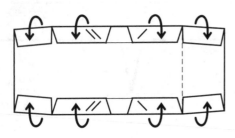

4. Valley fold right tab.

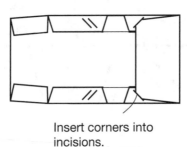

Insert corners into incisions.

5. Glue on cat (#28) or squirrel (#29).

Cat   Book cover

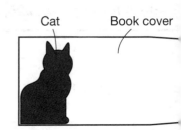

Flip over cover. Cut textured paper to patterns from p 55 and glue to left side of cover.

6. Wrap cover around book.

Paperback

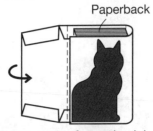

Insert cover of paperback into right pocket of book cover. Wrap cover around book and mountain fold left side to fit book. Insert folded tabs on left side and slide in other cover of book.

7. Make bookmark.

#28

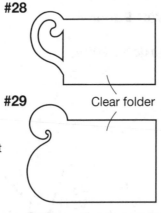

#29

Clear folder

Cut according to patterns on p 55.

8. Done!

#28

#29

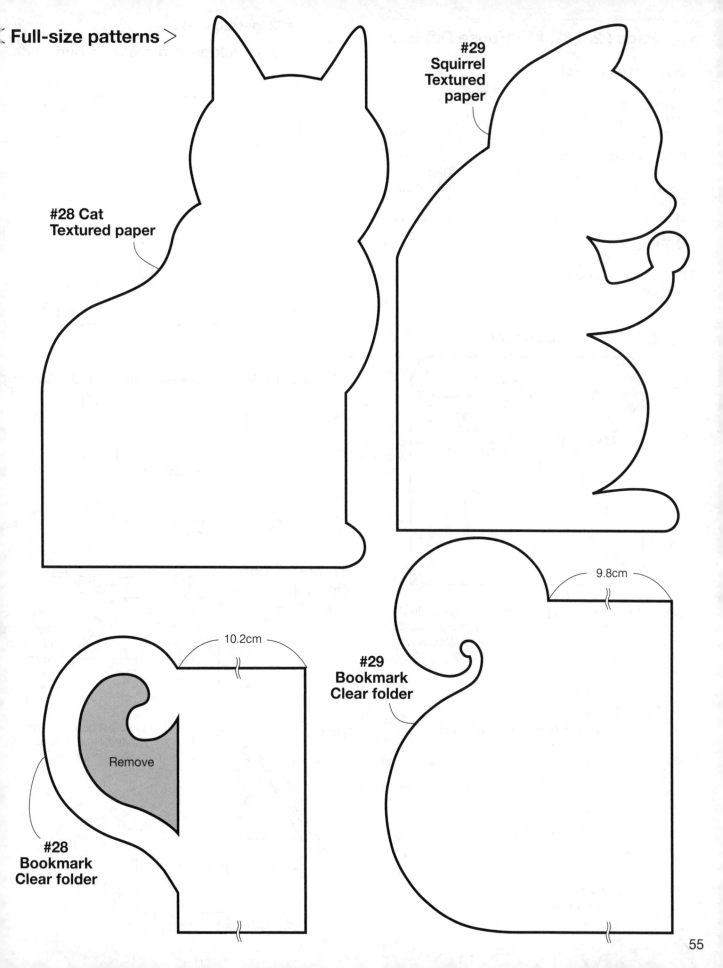

< Full-size patterns >

**#29
Squirrel
Textured
paper**

**#28 Cat
Textured paper**

**#29
Bookmark
Clear folder**

9.8cm

10.2cm

Remove

**#28
Bookmark
Clear folder**

Page 22, #32, #33 House Gift Box

● #32 Materials ●

Envelope	Kaku #4 (8 x 10.5")	Beige	1
Posterboard	6 x 29.5 cm	White/gray	1
Ribbon (3 mm wide)	1 m	Red	1
Masking tape	1/2" width	Green check	1 roll

● #33 Materials ●

Envelope	Kaku #6 (C5)	Beige	1
Posterboard	5 x 25 cm	White/gray	1
Ribbon (3 mm wide)	25 m	Red	1
Masking tape	1/2" width	Red check	1 roll

● Tools ●

Craft knife   Glue
Cutting mat   Spatula
Scissors

2. Attach masking tape.

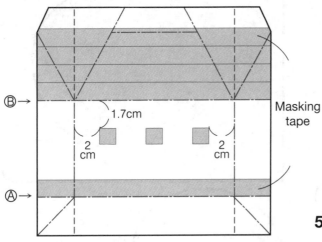

Place 1 strip of tape above line Ⓐ and 4 above line Ⓑ, aligning check pattern and circling over to the reverse side. Cut three 1.5 x 1.5 cm pieces and place only on front to create windows.

3. Fold up.
Fold down bottom triangles.

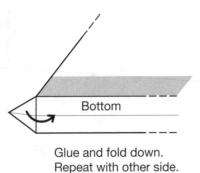

Glue and fold down.
Repeat with other side.

< #32 Instructions >

1. Cut envelope and crease along folds.

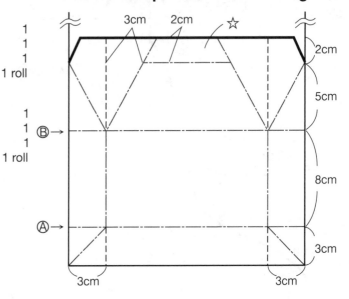

4. Fold posterboard and place inside envelope

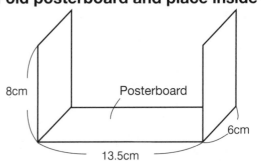

5. Thread ribbon through ☆ section.

Knot ribbon at right side and thread one end through ☆ section.

6. Done!

After folding in the ☆ section, thread ribbon through the other side as well and tie into a bow on the left.

Fold envelope

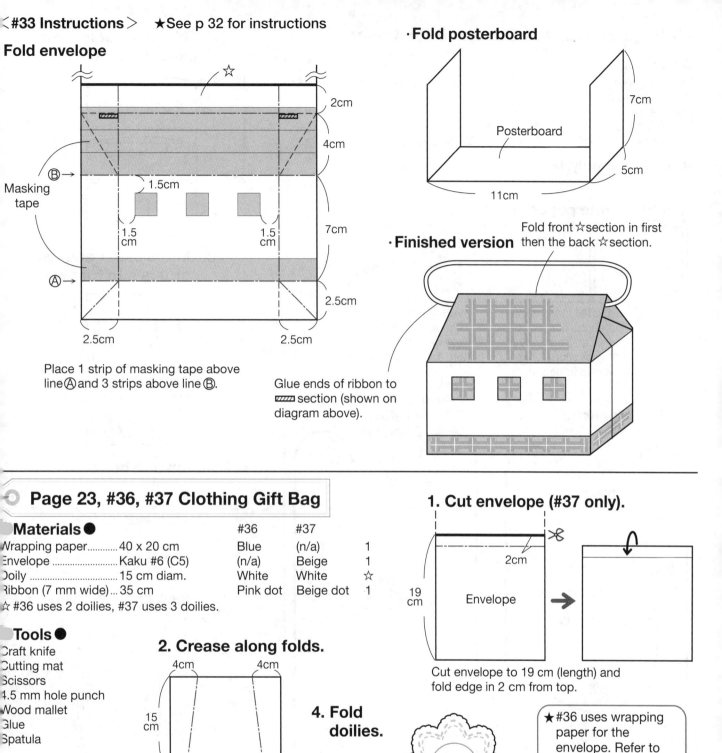

· **Fold posterboard**

Posterboard

7cm

5cm

11cm

Masking tape

2cm

4cm

1.5cm

1.5 cm

1.5 cm

7cm

2.5cm

2.5cm

2.5cm

Place 1 strip of masking tape above line Ⓐ and 3 strips above line Ⓑ.

· **Finished version**

Fold front ☆ section in first then the back ☆ section.

Glue ends of ribbon to ▨ section (shown on diagram above).

Page 23, #36, #37 Clothing Gift Bag

▌Materials ●

		#36	#37	
Wrapping paper	40 x 20 cm	Blue	(n/a)	1
Envelope	Kaku #6 (C5)	(n/a)	Beige	1
Doily	15 cm diam.	White	White	☆
Ribbon (7 mm wide)	35 cm	Pink dot	Beige dot	1

☆ #36 uses 2 doilies, #37 uses 3 doilies.

▌Tools ●

Craft knife
Cutting mat
Scissors
4.5 mm hole punch
Wood mallet
Glue
Spatula

3. Fold up. Fold down bottom triangles.

Bottom

Glue and fold down. Repeat with other side.

2. Crease along folds.

4cm   4cm

15 cm

2cm

2cm   2cm

1. Cut envelope (#37 only).

2cm

19 cm

Envelope

Cut envelope to 19 cm (length) and fold edge in 2 cm from top.

4. Fold doilies.

Fold both together and place over top of bag.

1.5cm

2cm

Ribbon

Use hole punch to open holes through all layers.

★ #36 uses wrapping paper for the envelope. Refer to p 59 for instructions.

5. Done!

For #37, cut last doily to make buttons.

● **Materials** ●

Favorite paper............................ 2x length, 4x width of book
(textured, wrapping, etc.)
Textured paper A .... 5 x 5 cm
Textured paper B .... 15 x 5 cm
Flat elastic (#30 only).............. 8 mm wide, 2x length of book

	#30	#31	
Favorite paper	Red	Light blue	1
Textured paper A	Gray	Gray	1
Textured paper B	Gold	Egg	1
Flat elastic	Black	(n/a)	1

● **Tools (#30 only)** ●

Glue

1. Fold favorite paper to fit book.

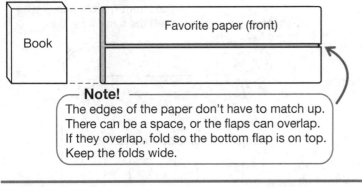

Book

Favorite paper (front)

Note!
The edges of the paper don't have to match up.
There can be a space, or the flaps can overlap.
If they overlap, fold so the bottom flap is on top.
Keep the folds wide.

2. Fold sides of favorite paper to fit book.

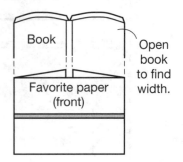

Book

Favorite paper (front)

Open
book
to find
width.

3. Unfold paper and fold corners into triangles.

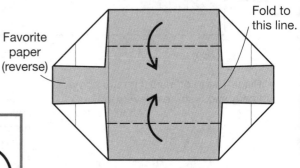

Favorite
paper
(reverse)

Fold to
this line.

4. Fold top and bottom.

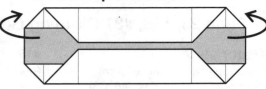

5. Mountain fold along side lines. Flip over.

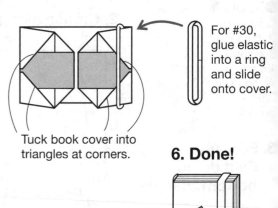

For #30,
glue elastic
into a ring
and slide
onto cover.

Tuck book cover into
triangles at corners.

6. Done!

Make bookmark
and insert into
front of cover.

<Full-size patterns>

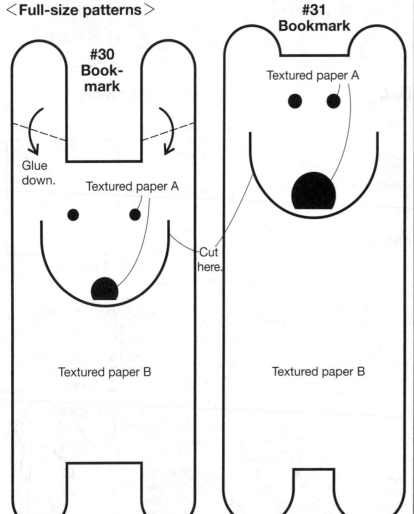

#30 Book-mark

Glue down.

Textured paper A

Cut here.

Textured paper B

#31 Bookmark

Textured paper A

Textured paper B

58

Page 23, #34, #35 Gift Bag

Materials ●

	#34	#35	
Envelope...............☆	Pink	Light blue	1
Doily...............15 cm diam.	White	White	1
Bristol paper...........B5	Dark pink	Blue	1
mm ribbon...........☆	Pink check	Light blue check	1

Envelope for #34 is Kaku #3 (8.5 x 11"); for #35, Kaku #2 (10 x 13")
Ribbon for #34 is 1 m; for #35, 70 cm

Tools ●

Craft knife
Cutting mat
Scissors
Double-sided tape (3/4")
Glue
5 mm hole punch
Wood mallet

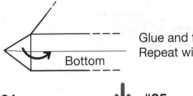
⟨Pattern: p 23, #36 ⟩

#36 Wrapping paper
Glue down margins
19cm
1.5cm   1.5cm
19 cm
16cm

1. Attach doily to Bristol paper.

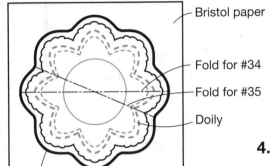

Bristol paper
Fold for #34
Fold for #35
Doily

Cut Bristol paper, leaving a 3 mm margin

2. Cut envelope.

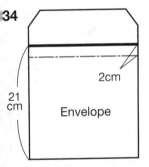
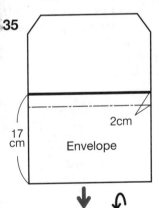

#34
2cm
21 cm
Envelope

#35
2cm
17 cm
Envelope

Fold edge in 2 cm from top.

3. Crease along folds.

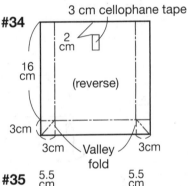

#34
3 cm cellophane tape
2 cm
16 cm
(reverse)
3cm
3cm   Valley fold   3cm

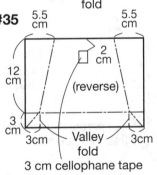

#35
5.5 cm   5.5 cm
2 cm
12 cm
(reverse)
3 cm
3cm   Valley fold   3cm
3 cm cellophane tape

4. Fold up. Fold down bottom triangles.

Glue and fold down. Repeat with other side.
Bottom

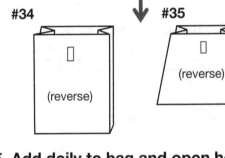

#34
(reverse)

#35
(reverse)

5. Add doily to bag and open holes.

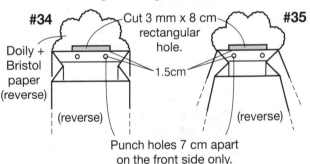

#34
Cut 3 mm x 8 cm rectangular hole.
#35
Doily + Bristol paper (reverse)
1.5cm
(reverse)   (reverse)

Punch holes 7 cm apart on the front side only.

6. Add ribbon.

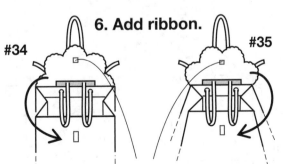

#34   **#35**

Place double-sided tape on the tab to align with tape on the bag when folded.

7. Done!

#34   **#35**

Tie ribbon into a bow.

Page 26, #39 Bathroom Tissue Box

● Materials ●

Posterboard.....................A3		White/gray	2 sheets
Textured paper A B3		Light green	1 sheet
Textured paper B...........B3		Purple	1 sheet
Textured paper C...........5 x 10 cm		Gold	1 sheet
Textured paper D...........5 x 10 cm		Bark brown	1 sheet
Round elastic 1			

● Tools ●

Craft knife
Cutting mat
Scissors
Double-sided tape (3/4")
Glue
Cellophane tape
Spatula
Craft punch
   (snowflake)

Tape ☆section to top
with cellophane tape
to make a cross.

1. Make box.

Cut posterboard
according to
diagram.

Cellophane tape

Fold up. Attach ends
with cellophane tape.

Cover outside of box vertically
with double-sided tape.

2. Affix textured paper B to box.

49cm

1.5cm

8 mm

Textured paper B

15 cm

Draw 2 guidelines.

Place double-sided
tape at right edge.

Peel off protective
paper and wrap in
textured paper B.

Cut perpendicular lines
into all 8 corners.

Glue and fold in
top margins.

Cut angles on
2 edges only of
bottom margins.

Glue and fold
down ① then
②margins.

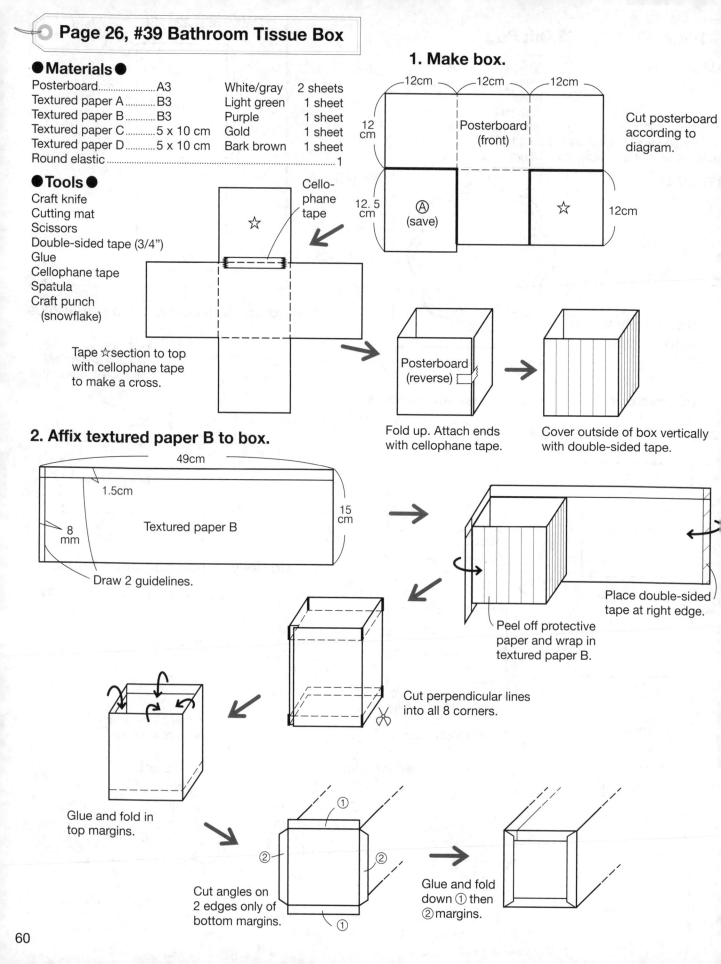

. Make case.

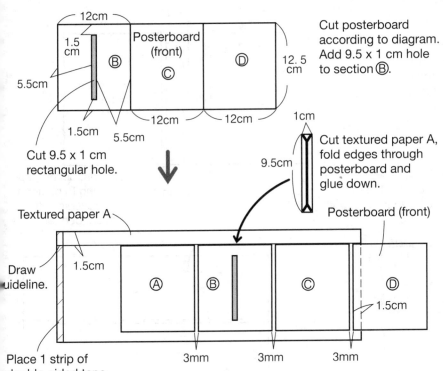

12cm

1.5 cm

5.5cm

1.5cm   5.5cm

Posterboard (front) ©

© D

12.5 cm

12cm   12cm

Cut 9.5 x 1 cm rectangular hole.

Cut posterboard according to diagram. Add 9.5 x 1 cm hole to section Ⓑ.

1cm

9.5cm

Cut textured paper A, fold edges through posterboard and glue down.

Posterboard (front)

Textured paper A

Draw guideline.

1.5cm

Ⓐ   Ⓑ   ©   D

1.5cm

Place 1 strip of double-sided tape at the left edge.

3mm   3mm   3mm

Cut textured paper A to 15.5 x 50.7 cm.
Attach section Ⓓ 1.5 cm from edge of textured paper.
Attach other sections of posterboard with double-sided tape from right to left, 3 mm apart.

© Ⓐ

D

Textured paper A

Fold into tube so section Ⓓ is next to section Ⓐ. The double-sided tape on the edge of the textured paper should stick to section Ⓓ.

Cut perpendicular lines into 8 corners of margins. Glue and fold down.

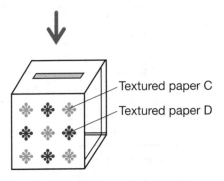

Textured paper C

Textured paper D

Cover backs of textured papers C and D with double-sided tape then punch out shapes with craft punch. Affix 9 each on two faces.

. Make spring.

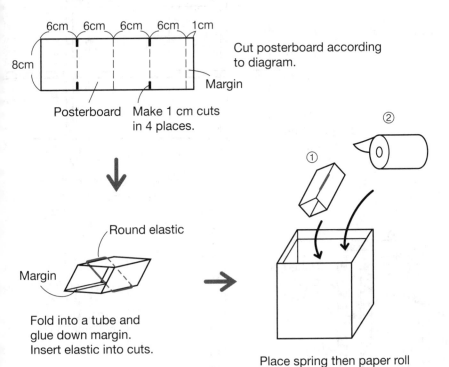

6cm   6cm   6cm   6cm   1cm

8cm

Margin

Posterboard   Make 1 cm cuts in 4 places.

Cut posterboard according to diagram.

Round elastic

Margin

Fold into a tube and glue down margin. Insert elastic into cuts.

①   ②

Place spring then paper roll inside box (with roll perpendicular to spring).

5. Done!

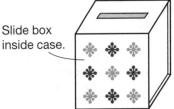

Slide box inside case.

Page 24, #38 Photo Frame

● Materials ●

Construction paper A3
Kraft paper A3
Patterned paper .... 30.5 x 30.5 cm
Ribbon A (1 cm wide) .. 70 cm
Ribbon B (1 cm wide) .. 17 cm

Gray	1
Light brown	2
Chocolate dot	1
Light blue	1
Light blue	2

● Tools ●

Craft knife
Cutting mat
Scissors
Double-sided tape (3/4")
Glue
Spatula

★ See p 63 for envelope instructions

Cut kraft paper to 28 x 30 cm.
Affix construction paper to kraft paper and cut off gray sections.

1. Make base.

11cm   2 cm   2 cm   11cm

Construction paper (front)   14 cm

3 mm   3 mm   3 mm

Cut construction paper according to diagram. Cover reverse with double-sided tape.

Draw 2 guidelines.

② 7cm

① Construction paper (front) ①   Kraft paper

28 cm

1.5 cm   1.5 cm

② 7cm

30cm

(front)

Glue and fold down ① then ② margins. Affix broad portions of ② with double-sided tape and glue down edges.

Ribbon A

(front)

Use glue 1 cm from edge.

6cm   Ribbon B   6cm

Affix B ribbons with double-sided tape according to diagram. Fold edges under. Affix ribbon A with double-sided tape so the center gap is concealed.

2. Make frame.

1.5cm
1.5cm

14 cm   Remove

Construction paper

11cm

Cut construction paper according to diagram. Cover reverse with double-sided tape. Make two.

Cut patterned paper to 15.4 x 12.4 cm. Affix construction paper and make margins according to diagram.

② ① ④ ① Patterned paper (reverse)

7mm

7mm

③ ③

② ④ 7mm

② Construction paper

7mm

Glue and fold down margins in numbered order. (This will become the reverse.)

Patterned paper (front)

. Affix frame to base.

Add glue, spacing 2 mm apart.

Glue in a C-shape pattern on back of frame and affix to base, aligning with inside fold of base.

(reverse)

Mountain fold   Mountain fold

Valley fold

. Done!

Insert photo from bottom.

(front)

When presenting as a gift, fold so photo is on the inside and tie ribbon into a bow.

＜Instructions for envelope＞

Slightly angle sides of margins.

7cm

2.5 cm | 15.5 cm   Kraft paper (B5)   2.5 cm

15.5cm

10cm

Cut out and affix patterned paper in any design, then fold into an envelope.

Page 27, #40 Pocket Tissue Box

Materials ●

Posterboard A3
Wrapping paper B3
Ribbon (1 cm wide)..35 cm

White/gray   1
Gray/red   1
Red/white check   2

Tools ●

Craft knife
Cutting mat
Scissors
Double-sided tape (3/4")
Glue
.5 mm hole punch
Wood mallet
Spatula

1. Make box.

6cm

Posterboard (front)

8.5 cm

6 cm   6cm

12cm

Posterboard (front)

Attach ends with cellophane tape

Cover outside of box with horizontally placed double-sided tape.

Cut perpendicular lines into all 8 corners.

. Attach wrapping paper to box.

42cm

1.5cm
1 cm

Wrapping paper (reverse)

9cm

Draw guidelines.

Place 1 strip of double-sided tape at right edge.

Draw 2 guidelines.

Peel off protective paper and wrap wrapping paper around box.

Continued on p 64

63

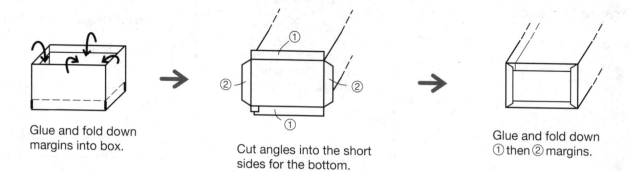

Glue and fold down margins into box.

Cut angles into the short sides for the bottom.

Glue and fold down ① then ② margins.

3. Make cover.

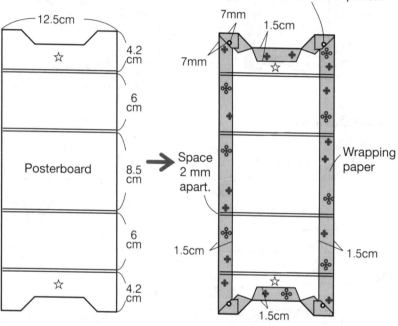

12.5cm

4.2 cm

6 cm

Posterboard

8.5 cm

6 cm

4.2 cm

☆

☆

Cut posterboard into 5 parts according to diagram. See full-size pattern below for ☆ section.

Open 4 holes with hole punch.

7mm

1.5cm

7mm

Space 2 mm apart.

Wrapping paper

1.5cm

☆

☆

1.5cm

1.5cm

Cut wrapping paper to 32.7 x 15.5 cm with 1.5 cm margins. Glue down margins. Affix other sections with double-sided tape. See full-size pattern below for margins pattern and glueing order of ☆ section.

4. Combine cover and box.

Place box inside cover. String ribbon through holes according to diagram and tie into bows.

5. Done!

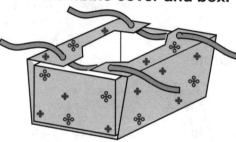

⟨Full-size pattern⟩

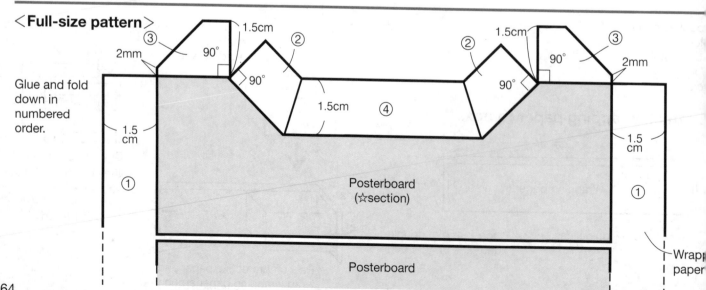

③ 2mm 90° 90°
② 1.5cm
② 1.5cm
③ 90° 2mm

Glue and fold down in numbered order.

1.5 cm

1.5cm ④

1.5 cm

①

①

Posterboard (☆section)

Posterboard

Wrapping paper